Destiny

put yourself first

Destiny

put yourself first

KARINA GODWIN

Destiny: Put Yourself First!
Karina Godwin

Destiny: Put Yourself First!
Copyright © 2017, Karina Godwin, All rights reserved.
A Flying Souls Publishing Book
www.flyingsoulspublishing.com
www.karinagodwin.com
Facebook: https://www.facebook.com/shineyourbrilliance/

First (eBook/paperback) edition: June 2017
Cover and Interior Design: Luke Harris, Working Type
Photography: James Havie
Edited by: Rebecca Wylie, Sage Written Word
ISBN: 978-0-648-06661-3

DEDICATION

To Nanny

*For being my everything and for showing me the gift that was me.
My world stopped spinning the day you died, and has never been the
same. It is your examples of generosity, kindness and forgiveness,
along with your passion for helping others that has inspired my work
as a healer and teacher, and therefore this book.*

Contents

Welcome!

How much do you love you?

Do you love yourself enough to put yourself first?

Or do you prioritise everyone else over your needs instead?

Are you so busy doing for everyone else,
that you can't see who you are?

Do you see yourself as a good person?

Are you critical of who or how you are?

Maybe you think you're fine, that you're doing fine.

I certainly did, but I was very, very wrong.

I couldn't see who I was,
my worth was framed by the words of others.

ᐧ

Do *you* realise just how wonderful you really are?

What if I told you that the world is a better place
because you're in it?

What if I told you that you don't know
or realise what you bring to people?

What if your self-esteem has become distorted
because you can't see your value?

What if I could take you to the day after you died and you could
see the grief and loss left behind for all of the value that was you?

Did you think that you had made a difference?

Did you realise that you changed that waiter/salesperson/child's
life by treating him/her like a person?

Did you understand that no one really needed the things
you did for them, but if it meant being with you a little longer,
then they'd take it every time?

Did you understand that as you couldn't see your own light,
you can't see all the good that I can see in you?

For I can see your brilliance, and you, my love,
are so special to the world.

You make a difference and the world is a
much better place for your presence.

What if I could show you?

Would you come on that journey with me?

Would you be willing to love you ... to see you
and to embrace your true brilliance?

Hi, my name is Karina Godwin and I have the best job in the world! I get to help people become happier and healthier and it all comes so easily to me. Each morning I wake up happy to embrace the day and all it holds. I find it difficult to say I'm going to 'work', because I just love what I do. Every day is different; every client or student provides new opportunities to create new wisdom and techniques, and the results have been incredible.

I created the Flying Souls Institute of Healing in 2003 as a source of workshops, classes and programs in personal growth. It provided the perfect opportunity for me to create the Meliae Intuitive Healing modality, which became our signature healing, and has been taught since 2005. Meliae means to change, to make better, and it combines the best healing tools with a powerfully intuitive energy healing experience, working to heal issues, symptoms and disease from their causative origins. Clients regularly improve their happiness, health and opportunities by focusing their healing on physical and emotional issues, relationships and productivity.

I've written this book to give you the opportunity to change the way you live. I want you to experience all the happiness that I have, all the happiness that has evolved through my journey with cancer. I've always been able to see more in others, and have created a myriad of ways to help change what's not working. That is why I share my stories with their secrets and shame with you. For what I can see in you, I have seen in me and in so many others. There's so much more in life that you could be experiencing, particularly as you learn to love yourself more. Life becomes happier with every tiny change.

I believe I got cancer for a reason. A whole heap of reasons actually, yet the most powerful is the birthing of this drive to help *you* make *your* life better. Not only better, but amazing. Watching you grow makes my heart sing with joy.

We are at the beginning of a journey, but one that many people have travelled with me before you. You'll be healing without even realising it as you read and experience these words, thanks to those who walked before you. A woman called Alesa had the most dramatic transformation which birthed my passion for working to increase self-esteem, self-worth and self-love in others. My clients literally transform before my eyes every day. It took me eight months to work out how I could bring the results of our healing rooms and classrooms into a book and have them work. I am so excited at what you can create!

If you could just see how brilliant you truly are!
For that is the truth of you.
That is the truth of who I am.

Each of us is brilliant beyond our imagination ... without exception!

I'm publishing this book to share with you for a reason. I want to give you the opportunity to ensure a life like mine never happens to you. I'm sharing a very personal story and there are others who have walked this path with me. It's not a book of blame towards them or of deflecting accountability for my own choices. It's a book of clarity. It's an understanding of how I got to cancer, and what contributed to my life becoming so toxic that it would be reflected in my body.

You'll find yourself in the rawness of the trauma of the cancer one minute, and in the next, in the events that led to creating it. It'll feel like you're walking hand in hand with me as I deal with the trauma, and then transform myself from the girl who created the cancer into the woman who could stand up and shine her own brilliance, happily making her destiny a priority for the first time.

You will have plenty of opportunities to create your own transformation as I've provided you powerful techniques, recipes for life and guided healing meditations.

Now is a great time to make things better.

I believe that was the purpose of my cancer; to stop me in my tracks, to teach me to receive and to show me what I was missing. In fact, what we're *all* missing. If we can't love who we are, then we can't forgive ourselves, and by default, we will struggle to forgive others. Our capacity to love and be loved will diminish or disappear. Our capacity to feel joy and to be joyful will also be depleted.

I have been healing for long enough to know that we can change this, that it doesn't have to be that way. My cancer gave me the gift of 'learning to receive', and I am finally putting myself first.

That is what I want for you—to love yourself enough to say 'yes' to you first! To say 'yes' when you mean 'yes', and 'no' when you mean 'no'; to honour that which your soul yearns for.

Don't worry that this is a book and you're not seeing me in person as you work through the healing techniques. While it would be lovely for you to be under my nurturing hands, experiencing my good looks and great sense of humour ☺, the healing meditations I have created offer that same healing within, and complement the learning in the book. The more you do them, the more change you'll create.

We're in a technological age, but not everyone has access to smartphones, tablets, computers and the internet. I wanted to make this healing experience available to everyone who picks up this book, so if you can read the meditations, or someone else can read them to you, you can heal. When you understand the content, you are halfway there, and the meditations will work on the rest.

Each of the meditations is written almost exactly as if they were recorded for the digital and CD versions. This way, you can record them yourself, memorise them or find someone to read them to you. If you'd prefer to listen to them in my voice, you can download them via your favourite online music stores. Search for *Destiny: Put Yourself First Guided Meditations*. We also have a companion CD for those of you who prefer a hard copy.

The great news is that you can get a FREE digital download of the first meditation as my gift to you.

To download this meditation, please go to the products/shop page at www.karinagodwin.com. Follow the instructions on the screen, add to cart and proceed to the checkout to collect your download. This offer is not limited to the original purchaser of the book. Feel free to share it with those you care about.

If you're unsure how to read a meditation, the free track will demonstrate how the meditation should sound. Just remember to speak it slowly and gently.

It's important to do the meditations regularly as prescribed (or at least as often as you can) to create the healing. You'll get where you want to go a whole lot faster, which is what they're there for!

Lastly, when you're reading the meditations, they may not appear to make sense.

This is intentional.

In creating the healing in each of these meditations, I am bypassing the ego and speaking directly to the soul, to facilitate the most powerful and proficient healing possible. It's a funny way of speaking, but the words of the meditation are music to the part of your soul that is hurting.

I'm just so excited, I can barely breathe! You're about to find out what living a life of loving you is like! I'm so full of my own love that it constantly spills over with joy into my everyday existence. It's just so damn exciting that this could be you too!

I wish you could see through my eyes what I've created for you. It took me eight months to work out how I was going to achieve actual healing through a book. Most of us know that it is almost impossible, but I love a challenge and here we are!

I know it can work, so let's get moving!

x Karina

Diagnosis Cancer

Busy, busy, busy.

Will there ever be a day when I manage to get everything done and have some time for me? I don't need a lot, just a night or a day off from the pressure of everything would be great.

There is just so much on!

I've had the most incredibly busy year. I always seem to be running late, rushing from one thing to another, every single day. There's just no space or time to take a break. I can't even remember the last time I had a haircut.

Although, if I'm truthful, it's not just this year. Every day of the last few years has been like this. Despite two of our five children moving out of home, I'm still crazy busy, but isn't everyone? I'm not the only woman running that fine line of trying to balance being a working mum.

The pressure builds because the option of being less than perfect just so I can give myself a break *isn't* an option. I can't handle the idea of one of the kids having missed another party, or being in the wrong uniform or costume for school one more time. More failure is just not an acceptable option for me.

Of course, the reality is that I'm *not* a failure. I'm also running a business which consumes a lot of my brain space, even if I'm not physically there. Being always available and on call can take a lot of energy, and right now, that is something that I just don't seem to have. I can't even seem to make it through the day. I'm always so tired—I even wake in the morning tired—but then I don't ever manage to get an early night. There's just so many people in need and so much to do.

I don't mean to make it sound like a disaster, because really, I have the most wonderful life in every other aspect. I admit that I'm overcommitted, but I'm working on it. I found my soulmate after a failed marriage and have never been so happy. Every day I'm surprised by just how much I love him, and how much that love seems to grow. Love with Berni is ever surprising. I never in my wildest dreams imagined that it could be this amazing; to be in the centre of someone's heart. My own heart seems to sing in response every time he's in the room. It sounds so soppy, but he's got some sort of magic with me.

We have five children who have brought us such great joy and heartache, along with headaches and sleepless nights and stress … but that's kids. I'm proud of how well we've done as a family to merge and connect with each other. I forget that I've only given birth to three of them, as the other two seem like they've been mine forever. I have so much love for them all and feel so humbled to have a place in their lives. Two working, one taking a gap year from university, one in the last year of school and a nine-year-old keeps things mighty interesting! I never know who'll be home for dinner.

Work is great too. I run a business, and it's the best business ever! My teaching, healing and psychic abilities were popular right from the start. It was just me, initially, but when I couldn't keep up I created the Flying Souls Institute of Healing to meet the demand. I dreamed big and started it huge.

That was not my greatest move!

With a one-week old baby and a very steep learning curve ahead of me in business, well, it's fair to say I was out of my depth. My expertise has always been in the health, wellbeing and happiness areas of life, so the business stuff stretched me past my limits. We downsized a couple of years ago to a beautiful little centre facing the beach in Melbourne. Now, we're in a beautiful place with less staff. It was life-changing for me! I went from incredible stress to making it work financially. I started to love going to work again.

Still, life is crazy, despite working so hard to simplify and clear out the stress, worry and overwork from my life. After downsizing the business, I started encouraging the kids to be more helpful and independent rather than doing everything for them, and I have tried *really* hard to be more organised.

I'm supporting my body more by getting regular healings, massages and exercise, but the exercise has actually become more of a problem than a help. While I walk away feeling fantastic (those happy hormones are awesome), my body does not hold up so well. My shoulder has been terrible after a bout of frozen shoulder reappeared a few years ago. Between weekly chiropractic sessions and myotherapy, I'm managing to cope with the problems that my back and shoulder raise after every exercise session. I think I've tried all different types of therapy over the years. I've used rehab trainers, chiropractors, physiotherapists and so the list continues. I just want to be able to go for a run with my little dog, Jack, and feel good for the rest of the week! Why is that so much to ask right now?

Today is one of those busy days. I've got breaky with the girls then myotherapy, I need to walk the dog, do some admin stuff, shop for dinner, and finalise Maddie's birthday present. It's a crazy day today with so many pressing things, but I'm trying to prioritise my health. Actually, it's just too busy today. I cancel shopping and decide we'll go out for dinner.

Breakfast is at a local café with my beautiful friends of eleven years. Our daughters were all in the same grade at school. The friendship has never abated, and the seven of us are still meeting on and off for breaky most weeks of the school year. There's always one of us with something happening personally, work-wise or with one of our children. We've developed such a great friendship, and we're such a strong support for each other that breaky is a priority for 'me' time. We're so busy chatting that I almost forget to leave for my myotherapy appointment.

Kevin, my myotherapist, is not a big guy, but boy does he pack a lot of power in his small hands. I've been seeing him for about a year now, and we spend my whole session chatting. My life seems to be very entertaining, and as he's seen almost all of our kids, a number of friends that I referred, and of course, Berni, there's always lots to chat about.

He greets me with a big smile and asks how I am. I tell him that I'm so tired today, and as always, crazy busy.

"I don't know how you do it all, Karina," he says with his big grin, as he leaves the room for me to change. I smile back wondering exactly the same thing.

Lying on the massage table, I have this real feeling of discomfort as I lay on my front. I've noticed it over the last few weeks when I lie down; it almost feels like a small water balloon in my belly. As I readjust my body so it's more comfortable, I again berate myself for having such a big breakfast before a massage session. The food must be sitting there in a huge lump.

Kevin sets about arranging the towels and puts his hands on my back. Straight away, he intuitively feels that I should have my back done rather than just my neck and shoulders. Who am I to argue? Everything has been tender since my personal training session earlier in the week, so I readily agree. He's chatting away, telling me how tight my muscles are, as he glides his hands firmly up and down my back.

Suddenly, I arch up off the table in agony.

Woah!

What was that?

He's asking me if I'm okay, but I can barely hear him through the pain. I'm literally shaking on the inside. I don't know what just happened, but I know immediately that this isn't good.

I readjust my body as Kevin fusses over me, trying to ensure that I'm okay. As he continues to chat and massage my back, neck and shoulders, I'm distracted by an increasing sense of internal dread. My inner knowing is that something is really, badly, terribly wrong. My nursing brain—developed through fifteen years of experience, including years in a large referral hospital—kicks in and I find myself running through possible scenarios. I don't like the sound of any of them and I don't like how my body is feeling either. It's so tender inside me.

I just want to get home to check out this sinking feeling I've got inside.

Could my nightmares and visions over the past three years be true?

I live five minutes away from the myotherapy practice, and I'm stripping off my clothes as I walk in the door. I stand in the bathroom naked, take a big breath and focus on the left side of my abdomen under my ribs, where I experienced the pain and also the balloon feeling. I've been palpating bodies as a nurse for long enough to know that I should lie down to do it properly, but it's like I'm in a daze and time is standing still. I'm not thinking, not doing anything, as I gently place my hand on my abdomen.

No!

I feel a hard lump and I know it's big and I know it's bad.

I don't even have to push hard, it's abundantly obvious. There's a huge lump in there. It's massive!

My breath is coming short and shallow and fast.

I've been nursing long enough to know how bad it is. The position is right on the pancreas and it's really hard. I lie on the bed and try again, checking it the right way this time, hoping against hope that I'm mistaken, and that it was a rib or a dream or anything other than what I fear.

There's no mistaking it. It's there and it feels like a giant mango-shaped rock.

I know without doubt that I am in trouble.

As I touch it carefully with my hands, I can also intuitively feel every cell of it, and it feels like cancer. During my years palpating tumours as a nurse, only the most aggressive cancers have felt this way. My medical knowledge reminds me that if this is pancreatic cancer, it will be bad.

By the size of it, I'll probably have less than a month to live.

I'm still hoping I'm imagining it, that this is a dream. Lachy, our eighteen-year-old son comes into the bedroom to ask what's wrong. It appears I've been crying. I get him to feel it too and his estimation of size is the same as mine.

OMG what is happening here?

I reassure him that I'll see the doctor today and we'll get it sorted. I phone for an urgent consultation and am relieved there is an after-hours appointment with a doctor at the local clinic. I don't know the clinic, as I'm so rarely sick that I haven't seen a doctor since we moved here.

Just three hours to wait ...

As I go to school to pick up Zavier, I toy with the idea of not telling Berni what's going on until I know for sure. He's not so fabulous when it comes to medical things, but as if he can hear my thinking, he's calling me. I live life without lying, and I know that when he hears the diagnosis he'll be devastated that I didn't trust him enough from the beginning.

He is silent when I tell him I've found a large lump and insists on being at the appointment with me. He immediately knows this is serious. Maybe it's the tone of my voice as I struggle to keep the fear out of it, or the fact I rarely go to the doctor. I can usually heal my symptoms successfully without needing medical intervention.

Berni is pale as he walks into the surgery, no doubt mirroring my own lack of colour. I'm trying to seem normal for Zavier, but on the inside, I'm somewhere between a full-on panic and the resignation that I'm looking at cancer.

Despite meeting him for the first time, the doctor is honest and compassionate. His face tells the story straight away. There's an unspoken communication between doctors and nurses that explicitly says that this is bad. He examines me silently for some time. When I ask him for his opinion, he reluctantly tells me it could be pancreatic. As he writes out the request for an urgent CT scan for the morning, I focus on his every word and expression, trying to keep my breathing regular. I glance at Berni and he tries hard to smile at me in reassurance. It couldn't be more obvious that he's very scared.

We go to dinner, talking quietly. Zavier is a typical nine-year-old and is excitedly making the most of my noise-cancelling headphones during this unexpected extra time he has been allowed to play on his iPad. First at the medical clinic, now at dinner; this is a very happy day for him!

We talk through the possibilities as Zavier cannot hear us. I'm as honest with Bern as I can manage, despite the fear stirring in my gut. When it comes to medical issues, we have always agreed that unless I'm worried, he can relax and I'll take care of things. My nursing and healing backgrounds, along with my highly attuned psychic awareness, means I'm great with medical and emergency type situations.

I look at him across the table in the ambient light of one of our favourite restaurants and tell him the truth. "Bern, I'm worried. This is not good, not good at all." I tell him about pancreatic cancer and how its prognosis is usually terrible. This is because by the time you get symptoms big enough to diagnose, it's usually quite advanced. It can happen in as little as a couple of weeks. It's terribly sobering and we go home to cuddle on the couch.

Lachy knows now too. He's waiting for us at home. He's studying PE and biology in his final year of high school, which means he understands more than he should. He's pale, yet I reassure him we'll wait till we get results. I gingerly explore the tumour as Bern makes a tray of tea. Now that I'm less panicked, I find that it doesn't feel like pancreatic cancer after all, which is a relief. Years of being sensitive to energy and working in big teaching hospitals have given me the opportunity to feel lots of different types of tumours. While it doesn't feel pancreatic, at this stage I'm so scared that I can't rely on anything I'm feeling.

As we get into bed, I realise that the frequent visions and dreams I've had over the last three years of having abdominal cancer are coming true. In fact, even as a nurse I felt that I would get cancer. Today, my reality has caught up with my visions, and not for the first time, I curse being psychic. Being the first to know doesn't seem to have helped me here at all.

I think of the tests I've had for my varying symptoms over the years and how they've all come back negative. I think of the CT scan two and a half years ago that showed this area to be clear. They found a growth in my pelvis which they attributed to endometriosis, and therefore was unlikely to be cancerous.

Oh ... but that's the wrong area of my body.

I can't breathe.

All of a sudden, I feel so overwhelmed.

The tears start flowing and Berni folds me into his arms to comfort me. He too has tears in his eyes when I look at him, and I feel so guilty and so scared.

I don't know what to do to make this better for him, or for me, or—

Oh no! What will I tell the kids?

What if this kills me?

My mind is racing. I can't sleep. I realise this is nothing new. I've been having trouble sleeping for months, dreading the nightmare of this exact situation. Sleep has not come easily in quite a while.

Saturday arrives and it's my daughter Maddie's twentieth birthday, although it's hard to believe that it is true. It's like I blinked and she was grown. We're meeting for brunch to celebrate with the five kids and their partners. Berni, Zavier and I arrive late due to the CT scan. We told Zavier that I've found a bad lump in my tummy and we need to get some tests to find out what kind of lump it is. It was such a difficult conversation to have without showing my fear or bursting into tears. Both Bern and I are trying hard to hide it, and we've decided to keep it quiet for today. I don't want to wreck Maddie's birthday; it needs to be celebrated.

It can wait till later. The test results will be back in a couple of days, although I can't shake this feeling of anxiety. I *know* the phone will ring, as they're unlikely to wait with what I assume they'll find.

Just as the food arrives, my phone starts to ring and as I suspect, the screen tells me it's the medical clinic. I step out to take the call—it's the doctor who is covering the weekend. He apologises for calling, but he needs to talk to me about my scan. When he acknowledges my nursing background in the next sentence, I know my worst fears have been confirmed. I'm trying so hard to breathe and focus on what he's saying. He gives me the results straight. "You have a large liposarcoma and I'm sure you know what that means. Do you want me to explain it to you?"

I ask him to read me the radiology report and I know I'm in worse trouble than I thought. This is a very rare form of cancer, and unless I'm mistaken, there's little or no treatment outside surgery.

His voice snaps me back to the present. "Karina, are you there? Is someone with you? Are you okay? Can you go straight to the hospital? I'm sure you understand the seriousness of these results. We need to get you to a surgeon and an oncologist as soon as possible."

I tell him that we're celebrating Maddie's birthday and that I'll go immediately after lunch.

I'm trying so hard to breathe, but everything is spinning. What is happening? Is this a dream? Am I dreaming right now? I pinch myself hard but nothing is happening. I'm still standing in the street with the phone in my hand and Bern is standing beside me, although I didn't see him come outside, and I have no idea how long he's been there.

I tell him I have cancer. It is not pancreatic, it's probably liposarcoma and with the size of the tumour, it's likely that it will kill me.

He takes me into his arms and I'm trying so hard to stay present in my body. I'm overcome with terror. I let go when the world stops spinning and I can breathe again, furiously wiping my tears away. I tell him they want me to go to the hospital immediately, but we'll finish lunch. The kids are not to know today. I will not spoil Maddie's birthday.

As soon as we sit down, I can see the kids know something is seriously wrong. I never take phone calls during meals, although I'm sure our faces tell a thousand words. Lachy is as white as a ghost, no doubt assuming the worst. It's obvious we have both been crying and despite my protests that we can't talk about it on Maddie's birthday, she insists. I look at the fear on their faces, and particularly at Lachy, and choose to tell them.

"I found a big lump in my abdomen yesterday that looks pretty bad. The CT results mean that I need to go to the hospital for more tests."

They're shocked, silent initially, but then they start questioning. I tell them it's likely we're looking at cancer, but we'll know more soon. They're such good kids, although really, they're adults, I guess. They rally together to support us and each other.

They gather up their little brother to go home so he's not exposed to the hospital. I whisper to Lachy that it's not pancreatic and he looks relieved. I look at Zavier's little face and tell him that the lump in my belly needs some more tests, this time in the hospital. Would he like to have a play-over with his older siblings? His innocence is lovely and it breaks my heart to see him so excited.

How much longer will I be able to watch his life—any of their lives? Dying is a very real possibility. I just want to scream at the injustice.

It's not fair!

As we drive to the hospital, I search through my memories of what I know of liposarcoma. I remember what I was taught and what I saw, and none of it is reassuring. Most people seem to die of this type of cancer, yet as I sought to still my breathing and let go of the panic, I feel certain I will not be one of them. I have the strangest and deepest sense of knowing that I will be okay, that this cancer will not kill me.

I have been working as an energy healer for years, and have had many opportunities to work with cancer patients, including my mother-in-law and sister-in-law, who have all survived. I see faces flash in front of me. I remember clients telling me that they'd beaten their cancers, one as recently as two days ago. I remind myself that not one has experienced a regrowth of their tumour or any metastases. I think of their vibrancy and aliveness, acknowledging their many paths to healing. Some combined my work with western medicine and others chose a more alternative path.

I take a breath.

I can do this. I can heal this. I will survive it.

Despite this inner knowing, it's hard to feel positive when the mood is so sombre at the hospital emergency department. No-one hides the truth if you are a nurse or doctor; there's an unspoken rule of transparency. As they draw blood, they speak of possibilities and the presence of a specialist team here in Melbourne for sarcoma. We're so lucky to have them. I walk away with referrals for an oncologist and surgeon I know I will never see. I can see the man I will work with—his name is David. All I have to do is find him.

We are both silent as we drive home. It seems we have stepped into an alternate reality. Is this real? Am I still dreaming? When we arrive home, it's clear this is not a dream. We need a plan, right now. We need to ensure that the energy around my treatment and recovery remains positive. Everyone and every moment will count, and have a direct effect on my ability to stay positive and focused. This is an important and essential factor in a successful recovery, and will be fed through people's attitudes and beliefs.

Bern and I know we need to keep the circle of awareness limited to those who can maintain a positive attitude, particularly through the battery of tests and specialist appointments that await me. We decide that less information delivered well is the best choice. It will be our approach for everyone—focusing on what is positive and leaving out the scary stuff wherever possible. Right now, we only tell the kids and those who can assist in my healing.

Through waves of grief and fear, we force ourselves to speak positively to the kids of what we know, determined to allay their fears regardless of what we've been told.

"The tumour is very large but appears to be contained. The scan shows there is no visible spread at this stage. This is cancer, but that doesn't mean it is a death sentence."

We ask them to keep the knowledge close and share it only with those they need for support. We need time to work out what we are dealing with and how. We are also mindful of what we need to do to manage the situation with my very large Australian and international clientele. I only want to be surrounded with positive healing energy, and worry will negate that. For some, this will be a crisis situation that will in all likelihood be experienced badly.

After the kids leave, we decide to share the knowledge with a couple of our close friends who are highly skilled Meliae Intuitive Healers.

Alesa and John are upbeat, positive in knowing that this is something I will conquer. They each begin to send healing to support me. We all know this tumour is something I will need to heal myself, yet I am grateful for their help in dealing with the fear, and ensuring my clarity and balance.

Peta and I nursed together many years ago. She's now a nursing manager and also a Meliae Intuitive Healer. My conversation with her is very different, combining what we believe and know spiritually, with what we know medically. She promises to use her contacts to find the most highly skilled doctor available in the country. I'm open to both healing and western medicine.

Di needs to know to support me at work, as she manages our healing centre and is also a Meliae Intuitive Healer. She too is shocked, but immediately positive that this can be cleared away.

I'm now in survival mode, knowing that every moment matters. Actioning my situation properly is critically important. I do not want the worry energy. We need to give me the best chance of healing the tumour while no-one really knows.

I set to research, to finding 'David', who turns out to be a sarcoma specialist at the big new cancer hospital right here in the city. I manage to get an urgent appointment the next day. David is gentle, clear, direct, respectful, and at the same time, very serious about the severity of my situation. He tells me there's not a lot of treatment for what is a very rare tumour, and that it is almost certainly malignant. We have a very big fight on our hands he says. "I only get one go at this tumour, it has to be done right."

I tell him of my job, of my psychic ability, of my dreams and visions of this cancer and my faith that we can beat it. He says he hopes so. He also approves me leaving for Hawaii at the end of the week, after first booking urgent scans and a biopsy. The trip was booked six months ago and is important to us as a family, but nowhere near as important as my survival. He reassures me that I have time to go, as all the tests need time to be processed.

We start managing the information, drafting releases to the staff and beginning to tell a couple of close friends and family. It is decided that we will wait until the biopsy results come back to tell everyone else. It is still on a need to know basis.

Scan after scan, bloods, and finally, an extremely painful and traumatic biopsy while packing for the trip keep me busy, but my attention is ever so focused on healing this cancer. I know from past experience that healing needs to be done using the innate healing and intelligence of the body. I need time.

Every day I have healing from my gifted friends. Every night Berni kneels beside the bed, gently rubbing pure Frankincense essential oil into my abdomen, and then he pours healing into both me and the tumour. The love and care that pours from him makes my heart sing and goes a long way towards allaying my fears. No matter what I am facing or have to do, he assures me he will be with me every minute of the way. His strength is surprising me, nowhere do I see his fear of anything medical. I hold on to him tight during the times when I can't feel my own strength and doubt my own ability to make this right.

I am scared beyond measure, yet it's the human part of me that's worrying. This is my least favourite part of my personality, and it takes me some time to take my attention away from this terrified voice. I breathe and meditate and go within and I find no fear inside, just a deep faith that I can beat this.

The part of my body that created this cancer has the same ability to un-create it.

I know that the same energy that holds up the stars and the sun and makes the gardens grow runs through me, and that it has the ability to heal. I have seen it over and over and over again. I remind myself of the success stories of the clients of Flying Souls, and of those around the world who have had stories of spontaneous recovery and healing from cancer.

I can do this. *Only* I can do this.

I am not sick because I have cancer, I have cancer because I'm sick.

Something in my energy is blocked. It has obviously been there for a long time for it to be affecting my body. I know how to heal this. I know there is a cause, and when I find it, I will be able to clear the blockage and release the energy so it can flow again. I know that if I can do this, it will enable the damaged cells in my tumour to repair themselves with time. If those same cells are healthy, they will replicate with new healthy cells. This tumour can be cleared of its cause, and then I can find the behaviours that fuel it and the recipe within my body that feeds it. Then I'll make a plan to address them too.

I know this can and will be done. I am choosing to live, I am choosing to watch my children grow through their lives, and to meet and watch their children grow.

This will not kill me!

I'm not working today and I need to work on the cancer straight away to ensure the healing has time to integrate throughout my body. These cancers are often very hard and while I haven't worked directly with a liposarcoma before, I'm assuming that it will take longer than a normal tumour to disappear. This is a very aggressive type of cancer, so it's also important to do the healing now to make sure that it doesn't grow any more, or move into any other areas of my body. Time is of the essence as we're leaving on Sunday for Hawaii. I need to go inside right now.

I lie on the bed, intuitively choosing from the huge number of healing crystal stones in the house to cover my body. I intuitively reach for my Young Living essential oils and apply those that will assist in the healing, in my recovery, and enhance my clarity and ability to see and heal.

I feel a great peace come over me as I breathe away the fear.

I feel myself becoming very 'spacey' as I move into the healing awareness that allows me to see inside myself, and to see the spirit world.

Immediately, I see the room has been filled with angels and I feel so safe and sacred. I know in this moment that the cancer has not come as a death sentence. It is here as my teacher and it comes with a purpose—to assist me to teach others to nurture, to care for and to love themselves.

I breathe deeply again and I can see the tumour clearly.

It is much more calcified than I would have liked—the whole thing looks rock hard. I move slowly through the expanse of the tumour, looking for its core. Inside the core will be the secret: the pain, the trauma or the fear that has caused my energy to seize. That frozen state of energy has stayed locked inside because I wasn't able to, or couldn't, process what I experienced.

My vision changes and I am no longer in the room.

I see myself as a little girl in the kindergarten playground. I am watching a messy looking man in the adjacent park swaying towards us, a bottle in a brown paper bag dangling from his left hand. He doesn't seem able to walk properly. I don't know what's wrong with him, but I know that he feels scary and I don't like it. I want to go home to Nanny's house; she's at home just a few houses away. She's coming to collect me soon. Oh, I wish she was here now! She'd fix things. I'm not sure what he's going to do. He's leaning over the iron railings of the fence muttering unintelligibly. I call to my teacher and she immediately ushers us all inside.

Oh, I forgot my hat! Oh, no! I'll be in trouble!

I race outside to collect it, and see the senior teacher has approached the man and is ordering him to leave in her cross voice. She's gruff and firm, but he's not listening. He doesn't even care and she's the boss around here!

Oh, no! He's grabbed her between the legs, underneath her dress, and she's gasping in shock and fear and pain and horror. She doesn't seem able to move, but she sees me in that moment. I squeal in fear and run back inside, the hat forgotten. I run so fast. That's a bad man and he's going to get me next.

As I run, I feel water running down between my legs. I'm so scared. I run to the toilets and hide in the corner in terror and shame, tears pouring down my face. She finds me there after she's checked her face in the mirror, wiped away her tears and readjusted her skirt. She pulls me to her and I feel her breath and her heart is racing too. She tells me it's okay and she's okay and that I don't need to worry. I'm too scared to move and refuse to go back to the group. That's when she notices I've soiled myself. I feel my heart slowing and my breathing settle a bit as she cleans my face and changes my underwear.

Despite her reassurance, I can still feel her fear. I hear the voices in her head and I'm still terrified.

I can't handle it and try to push it down to my tummy so I can breathe again.

As we join the group, she sits beside me with her hand on my back. The two teachers exchange glances that I don't understand. I feel myself retreating inside, my heart shrinking in response.

As I'm breathing deeply, the vision fades and I can see that the terror is still living inside the core of the tumour. This is what I need to heal. The fingers of my right hand move intuitively, and there is the most beautiful and brilliant golden healing energy pouring from them into the core of the tumour.

I feel and watch the healing energy dissolve the buried emotion that warped the cellular structure during that traumatic time, enabling those damaged cells to replicate into a tumour. I know that if I can get to the source of the tumour inside, find that which created it, I can heal it. I know where to look, and am ever grateful for every client with cancer that has come to me for healing, and for every patient I observed energetically while nursing. Looking into their bodies has helped me understand how the energies of the body work, and how cancer finds its way there.

I am surprised at finding the cause to be in kindergarten, yet the repressed emotions of terror and shame of this forgotten incident are very real and massively overwhelming.

As the healing spreads, I move from feeling the terror as a little girl, to a sense of peace that tingles throughout my body.

I feel it release.

The healing energy works from my hands into the core of the tumour and I feel it begin to change. Still, it does not seem complete. There seems to be a stem of a similar issue still feeding it. I go deeper again, using my ability to search my past incarnations. I see a vision of one of those incarnations almost instantly. I have always easily returned to times past. It's like I never forgot them when I was born.

The golden healing energy penetrates even further, into the blocked energy sourcing from that time, and then I know I have healed the core. Its centre feels empty.

As I lay on my bed, nurtured by the healing crystals and essential oils whose aromas surround me and fill the room, I feel my body shift and move. The tumour has always felt like the worst type of sarcoma, yet it feels like it is changing, not shrinking exactly, but changing nonetheless.

I breathe in the sunlight streaming through the full-length windows, and I feel like I'm beginning again.

My belly is moving on its own, and as I watch, I remember my babies doing that to my belly as they moved around inside. I feel such joy and relief—it feels like I have dodged a bullet.

Yet I know that I am not done.

A tumour needs a cause, but it also need to be fuelled, and then it needs a catalyst to grow it. I know that work on this cancer still needs to be done, but I feel peaceful.

I know now that I have time.

I Hated Myself Sick

I just wanted to be loved.

As a young child, I always believed that if someone was angry at you, they had stopped loving you and therefore hated you. I couldn't bear the feeling that came with all their anger—all I wanted to feel was love. So, I'd get angry; angry that they were angry at me, and then angry that I *was* me. I'd match their hate with my own and direct it towards myself for being different to the other kids. Why couldn't they just be kind? Why did they have to yell or use bad voices?

I was a child with an ability to see into others, which came with a severe hypersensitivity to energy. When someone was angry, the anger felt like acid inside my heart, like it was breaking into a million pieces. I'd grab that feeling and push it away from my heart, down into my belly. Then I'd get angry at me for being so stupid and end up hating myself too. I'd try harder to please them and do anything to keep the peace, so I never had to feel that 'badness' again.

I hated myself SICK!

I didn't even realise how critical I was of me, how judgemental and how bitchy. I measured myself and my worth as zero. I never expected to be enough. I knew I was different, so I withdrew into myself so that no one would see me. I was shy and rarely attracted the praise of others, so there were few positive voices to argue with the negativity that was in my head.

When I measured myself against others—how they looked, how they laughed, how pretty they were, how funny—I was always less. Without question, I was always 'lacking'. I was surrounded by very pretty girls who wore lovely clothes and hairclips that my family couldn't possibly afford. I was surrounded by boys who spent an enormous amount of time laughing at everything around them. They delighted in teasing anyone and anything. I was a perfect target, particularly when I claimed a real-life angel had saved me from a paedophile in my first year at school. 'Angel Girl' I became.

I didn't like it and wished I could disappear, and my wish came true in the form of a change of school and a move of house. I was hoping I could start fresh, and be liked instead of teased by a new group of children. No one would know that I could see angels—I would tell no one. I was so hopeful when I walked into the classroom and saw the children smile at me. This was my chance.

As we settled into the day, my teacher told us of a very special project she had for us. She passed out large pieces of paper and thick crayons and asked us to draw what we wanted to be or do when we grew up.

Oh, what a wonderful place this was!

I drew and drew and drew and finished what I believed to be a masterpiece depicting a perfect world full of happy people. It felt like the Heaven my nanny told us about.

One by one we ventured up to the front to stand beside the teacher and explain our drawing. There were so many drawings of teachers and doctors and nurses and policemen and firemen and farmers. I was feeling positive and confident as I held up my picture. "I want to make people happy. I want to make them so happy that they don't want to hurt people, and they can say sorry. Then we can all live happily together." I looked expectantly at the class and was horrified to see their laughter.

Not one child had described a non-traditional role and I guess they thought I was silly. They certainly said so.

I could feel the tears welling in my eyes.

Not again!

I just want you to like me, to be my friend.

The teacher clapped her hands sharply and the snickering stopped immediately. She gave each child a stern look and said to the class that this would be the hardest job of all those she had heard today. She turned to me and said, "Karina, while this is a very difficult job, if anyone can do it, I believe that you can and will. Always believe that you can become whatever you want to become, that you can be what you want to be."

As I sat down in my spot on the carpet, a little girl moved closer to me and said she liked my job and my picture. I smiled gratefully and the class moved on.

Later in the week, the class did sport and this time it was cricket. Two captains were appointed and each of them got to pick their teams. Being new, I was the fourth last choice, with only those children picking their noses and looking disinterested left. I felt so deflated that it only served to compound the thoughts from the first day; that I wasn't as good as the other children.

Looking back, it's abundantly obvious that I should have looked to the teacher to source my self-confidence. Her behaviour that day gave me a foundation that would hold me together, but unfortunately, the laughter was ringing in my ears and the tears stinging my cheeks as the week wore on. I was a highly sensitive child. I felt everything and could even feel the pain inside those around me. The world was an entirely overstimulating place, so filled with negativity.

I felt ashamed that what was in my heart was so poorly received and the cricket only served to crystallise and amplify that 'lack' when I missed catching the ball. I had lost my confidence when I wasn't picked early for the team. If only I could have caught the ball, the kids would have liked me. Everyone loves the kid that's good at sport or who saves the game. Alas, my missed catch only served to ensure that my self-confidence spiralled downwards.

That day was the start of a very nasty habit of looking at the worst of my performance or behaviour, and defining myself as a loser as a result. No matter how well I did something, no matter how smart I was, I would feel the disappointment of not achieving the best.

When I found myself with a tumour, the first thing that jumped into my mind after the shock and terror of leaving my family without me, was disgust. Here I was, a healer, who was known for her incredible gifts and ability. I had international and interstate clients who came specifically to me for my healing gifts. I had helped people for well over a decade. There were clients who I had healed from incurable physical ailments and psychological difficulties that had persisted despite years of treatment and/or counselling. None of it seemed to matter now.

I had cancer.

How was that even possible? If I was any sort of healer, then surely that would never be true. How is it possible that I can see into the bodies of others and help them to heal or prevent serious diseases and injuries and emotional issues, yet I didn't prevent it or see it in myself?

But maybe that wasn't exactly true.

Many spiritual teachers of our time have suffered cancer as a wake-up call. How many of them stepped onto the path of spirituality as a result of their disease? And yet still I was sneering. "What kind of a healer and psychic are you? You're a fraud! You're a heap of shit! You're useless! You don't know anything at all! You're loopy!"

All of the negative voices of people in my past flooded up to fill my head and brain with disgust. Why had I not paid proper attention to that first vision on our holiday in Queensland? Maybe things would have been different.

I thought back to seeing myself with cancer for the first time. I was on holiday, staying in the most beautiful and isolated property in the Daintree Rainforest in Far North Queensland. I was standing in the bathroom and something I randomly said had made Berni angry. It wasn't even that important to me, but it obviously mattered a great deal to him. He walked out of the room with steam pouring out of his ears to the pool area to cool off. It rattled me to see him like that. I hadn't meant anything by it and I began to wonder if he did indeed love me. I was shaking, as it was so unusual for him to behave this way. Not only do we barely ever argue, we really enjoy everything about being together ninety-nine percent of the time. I felt something triggering inside of me, and my eyes were changing focus.

I'm still standing naked in the bathroom facing the mirror, when the image of my body disappears. I'm seeing myself looking at another smaller mirror in what looks like a hospital bathroom. I have pulled down my white hospital gown and I am trying to see a wound on my abdomen, stretching from my diaphragm to my pubic area. It has large surgical staples every 5 mm or so, holding together a massive surgical wound.

As I look up, I can see the IV pole is supporting me and its bags of fluids are connected to multiple tubes coming out of my arms. I also have two tubes coming out of my nose: one connected to a feeding flask and the other a drainage bag. I look at my face. It's tanned like I've been on a holiday, yet there is a pallor that speaks of being seriously ill. It's like time doesn't exist right now.

As I watch, I realise that I look much older in the vision and that the older me is in shock as she sees her reflection in the hospital mirror. I hear her saying out loud that she can't believe she has actually had such a huge cancer removed and they've gotten it all.

All of a sudden, everything goes white and I'm spinning, and the now is mixing with the then and I don't know where I am.

All I can feel is the terror, and the next thing I know I'm back, but I'm on the floor and Zavier is screaming out, "Daddy! Daddy! Daddy! Come quickly! Mummy's fallen down and there's blood!"

Berni is there in a flash and calling me, but his voice is fuzzy and things are spinning. I'm hurting in the places I've fallen. My face is throbbing around my eye, and I'm feeling gingerly for blood, to see if I've broken anything. Did I lose consciousness? Did that really happen? Oh, why do I have to be so psychic?

I know now that I have seen into my future and it's not good, not good at all.

∽

I hated myself for being psychic nearly every day of my life. I hated that it made me different, that people gave me that 'look' anytime something psychic slipped from my mouth. I was pretty good at hiding it away, which became a necessity as I found myself punished or ostracised for talking about spirits or dead people or what I could see in the future. So, I kept it quiet, which only served to increase my derision of my differences. It built upon what I felt that first day of my new school and created a toxicity in my attitude towards myself that could only be harmful in the long run.

I married my first husband despite years of visions of another man with my children. I was filled with a dread that this marriage wouldn't last.

After dinner that night, an intoxicated man tried to 'pash' me with his mouth open and tongue moving wildly toward my lips, instead of the expected friendly kiss on the cheek. As this man was well known to him, my fiancé refused to believe it could have happened. He assumed I must have mistaken the circumstances.

I couldn't believe it.

He had caught me off guard, but what girl hasn't learnt to recognise when a man wants a 'pash' versus a kiss on the cheek?

I was perfectly sober and the man was obviously inebriated. Why would I make it up? I had been on a high thinking of the wedding. Not anymore. My high was immediately gone and I couldn't sleep that night. I wanted out. He was adamant that my reaction was due to cold feet.

I knew within the core of my being that I was making a mistake.

I knew that this marriage could never last without him believing in me. Still, I allowed myself to be convinced, rather than risk the ire of those who were travelling far and wide for the wedding. He was difficult at times before we married, yet aren't we all? I knew I wasn't perfect and that this was probably a good offer for a girl like me.

I couldn't tell him or his family about my ability. His mother was deeply religious and she once told me that she believed psychics had the devil working through them. He'd told me before that psychics were a 'load of shit', brought about by fraudsters and charlatans. So, I became watchful. I was careful, mostly keeping quiet about what I knew and could see, living underneath their radar.

It wasn't like they were the only people who thought that way. I had birthed myself into a family and a community that was ill-equipped to understand my gifts. When I was born, it was still a taboo subject, a hidden and undesirable secret. I couldn't help what I knew and could see, but I also knew that I shouldn't let people see. Not only did I hide it, I hated myself for doing so every day.

As time wore on, the traumas I faced as a child would cement the hatred I felt for myself. I was pushing the pain I was feeling into my belly to insulate it, right at the spot where my tumour would later appear. Over and over, I would do it again and again to protect myself from each new, unresolved pain.

‿

When I heal others, it's very clear to me that how you feel about yourself creates a terrible toxicity within the energy of the body. Japanese scientist Masuro Emoto published a book called *Messages of Water* where he described his experiments of emotions upon water and the resultant molecular changes in the water, which were then photographed. When water was exposed to negative emotion, the images were static and unattractive. Beautiful images resulted when the water was exposed to words like 'love' and 'gratitude'. Our bodies are predominately made of water, so it is no surprise that based on his findings, the molecular structure of the body could be affected by the negativity that you or others inflict upon it.

In hating myself, my body became acidic, turning my silver jewellery black, and eventually feeding the capacity to create the tumour. In burying the pain of my trauma for decades, my body reacted by changing its cells. I would never have imagined that becoming frustrated, impatient and negative towards myself could have such disastrous outcomes.

I didn't have time for me. I was super busy all the time. There was always someone with a problem and I felt like I was obliged to help them. If you feel bad about yourself, helping other people can take that feeling away. Watching their relief or happiness grow makes *you* feel better. If you had the cure for something or the ability to prevent an adverse outcome, shouldn't you fix it? So, I did. Whenever, wherever they needed it, whoever needed it. I spent large amounts of time each day and even during the night, healing directly or globally, as it was needed, and because I could.

I spent hours on the phone counselling people on their latest issue or drama. I hated to see people in pain, so I did what I could to take it away. As it turned out, I could do an awful lot to take away pain, so I did it some more, and then even more again. Why should people suffer if I could stop it happening or ease it?

The lack of sleep took its toll, and I stopped seeing the bigger picture. I became very focused on the moment. It was as if I were 'putting out fires' everywhere.

I stopped prioritising my needs and I stopped noticing what was happening underneath my nose. I was shattered to discover that I'd ignored my own body's needs so much that it was too depleted to fight the creation of a tumour.

It was abundantly clear that my lack of self-care had contributed to the cancer growing in my body. My behavioural choices meant that I had inadvertently nurtured the perfect conditions to grow cancer.

The life I was leading had to change, and quickly. I needed to learn how to put myself first and listen to the yearnings of my body or things would never be right.

I felt like I was looking down the barrel of a loaded gun. If I listened to the nurse within me, I was likely to die. It was hard to listen to anything else.

I was beside myself at the idea of having cancer, let alone the reality that it was not a dream anymore.

Action!
The Power of the Breath

I was asked yesterday about the secret to my success and it took me no time to answer. Stillness creates everything I need. It amplifies my intuition and my ability to flow through life with ease and grace, rather than being bogged down with drama and issues. I'll talk more about stillness in chapter seven, but first we need to master the essential tool to achieve stillness: the breath.

We think of breath as being essential for life, knowing we can't survive without the oxygen it brings or the carbon dioxide it removes from the body. Without oxygen, there is no life, therefore breath is ever so important.

Yet for me, the breath brings so much more, and mastering it is the difference between living life and really enjoying life.

Breath acts as a drug, one that is intrinsic to all of the vital functions of the body, and which also feeds your state of joy. And that's the secret right there—the breath is the carrier of joy. You can't expect that you'll really love your life if your breathing isn't working.

I know it sounds a bit obscure, but think about it for a minute. When you exercise, you feel good, as all of those happy hormones bring about a feeling of wellbeing and enthusiasm for life. Even your tired and aching muscles can't get in the way of that, and you're keen to exercise again as it makes you feel good every time you do. When you're exercising, you're breathing a lot more and a lot faster. The body has a huge appetite for oxygen to ensure that the lungs and heart can fuel the muscles to enable your body to achieve peak performance.

One day, I was exercising with my trainer when it occurred to me that something interesting was happening as I watched the energies of the other people in the gym. I was surprised to see that the breath was fuelling more in the body than just its physical function. I could see the energy of the oxygen and the magic it appeared to be making. When I watched the patrons' enjoyment for exercise, it was *oxygen* that appeared to be fuelling this joy more than hormones. It appeared to me that the more you breathe, the happier you could be.

That started a fascinating period of watching oxygen, and what, if anything, it was doing in all of the different people I saw through my healing work, and around me as I walked through life. It was extraordinary the difference between those who were breathing deeply and consciously, and those who weren't. It was literally the difference between how happy people were and how anxious they weren't.

Breath and its benefits aren't a secret; monks have been using it to their advantage for thousands of years. It's just that we don't all have a breath master to help us.

I've taken what I've learned and noticed, and incorporated it into everything I teach. I encourage my clients to make their life different, *better*, using the simple exercises that I love, and with massive success. You'll see them scattered throughout this book, although they're most obvious in the meditation chapters. For you to get the most out of these exercises, it's worth taking a minute to master your breath.

There's so much that I love about the breath.

It's like a mute button for that negative voice in my head. I can literally take my breath and silence it. It's probably the most liberating thing I've experienced.

I simply breathe deeply and imagine I'm breathing into that voice so that it pushes its air backwards. No sound comes out, none! Neither does that nagging, whinging, critical and mean-spirited voice. It is brilliant. It gives me the space to gather my thoughts, to decipher the truth of my situation and to evenly make my decisions. I'm not using it to completely silence that voice as it does have its uses, rather I use it when it's out of control and I need space to think.

The breath is a trigger for the brain. How it is feeling and behaving can tell the brain whether to put you in the 'fight or flight' response in times of danger, or to relax in times of ease. When you're in danger, the body has a whole set of reactions that draw energy and blood away from non-essential functions of the body to give you the fuel to run or defend or escape the danger you find yourself in.

The problem with this is that many of us have slipped into the habit of living in the fight or flight state all the time. We worry and stress, and it lifts our breathing to become shallow and fast. This tells the body that there is danger and puts it into the watchful state. That is a big problem because the body is not designed to maintain this state, and if energy and blood aren't fuelling the digestion properly, you can create all sorts of digestive and weight problems in the body. Stress actually causes our digestion to deteriorate. If it isn't working well, neither is anything else, as you won't be drawing the nutrients from your food properly.

So, the first thing we want to do is to calm the mind to help the body achieve optimal functioning.

If we can separate ourselves from what is going on, we can settle the mind and body. Sometimes though, that isn't realistic, especially if you're panicked or worried or anxious about the outcomes, or the dangers, of all the aspects of your life.

So why don't we do it backward and use breath as the tool?

If you can master your breath, you can trick your brain back into the belief that you and your environment hold you no harm. The body will do what it does best and settle all of its functioning back to optimal levels for every part of the body. You just need to breathe properly.

Some of you may have tried yoga. They're really big on the breath. I remember my first class, and I honestly thought my lungs might actually explode with what they were asking me to do. I'd come from years of suffering from depression and my breathing was shallow and sharp. It's okay to feel awkward as you begin to work with your breath, it's a new skill and awareness that you're learning.

Let's take a moment here to check in with your own breath.

Where in the lungs are you breathing to? Is the breath going deep into the bottom of your lungs, or is it sitting somewhere high in the chest?

Your breath is supposed to fill your lungs, and if you've ever had surgery or a chest infection, you'll have had your doctors and nurses saying so. Your lungs look like an empty bunch of grapes. When you breathe deeply, you fill the entire bunch, including the bottom grapes for optimum levels of oxygen to enter the body. Each grape is like a little air sac. The more air you inhale, the more oxygen you have, and the more oxygen you have, the happier and healthier you'll be. If you fail to breathe deeply, the bottom sacs stay shut and have the potential to become sticky and infected, making you sick. There's so much to encourage us to breathe well!

When I'm upset, I stop and breathe. When I'm angry or when my many roles collide and I can't cope, I stop and breathe. When I upend my turmeric chai all over me, I stop and I breathe to bring myself back into balance. When I breathe, the breath and the process of breathing, centres my energy back into my body. It helps me gather my attention and focus on what's real and what I know, so that I can make great choices.

Breathing makes me more productive and it makes me a nicer person.

When I breathe, my body begins the processes in conjunction

with my mind to bring my body back into balance. When I breathe slowly and deeply, it tells my brain that I'm safe and I automatically slip into a state of greater clarity. I'm able to relax and look at things clearly while my body starts functioning properly again. Life isn't as hard when I do this, and I can stay more in the moment rather than stressing, so that makes me happier too.

When I breathe, I feel my body responding with joy and I feel happier. If I breathe deeper and deeper, more and more often, I am even happier. It's like I'm filling my joy tank.

So, how do we breathe for joy, peace and balance? Here's my recipe.

Recipe for Joy, Peace and Balance

1. Find a quiet spot and become aware of your breathing. How fast are you breathing? How regular? Is the breath warm? Is it the same temperature going in and out of your nose? Are you breathing through your nose or mouth? Don't try to control it, just become familiar with how you breathe.

2. When you breathe in, imagine breathing in a breath that is filled with joy that feeds your spirit. See it calming you and imagine that it is filling you up with joy.

3. When you breathe out, imagine the breath is gathering all that is negative in your mind and body and expelling it from your body. You feel lighter and lighter with every breath.

4. Imagine that your breath is like a gas, and that it can

pass through the limits of your lungs. Imagine the joy that is coming from the breath seeping out of your lungs and saturating all of the other cells and tissues and organs in your body. You're feeling so much happier with every breath.

5. Imagine now that the breath can heal. Imagine sending the breath past the confines of your lungs and into the parts of your body that are tight or painful. Imagine you can actually breathe there and as you do, it dissolves away or disintegrates those feelings, relaxing the tightness and relieving your pain.

6. Imagine now that you can see or feel dark patches where your negative emotions have gotten stuck: e.g. anger, sadness, grief, disappointment, rejection, judgement, irritation, frustration, guilt, blame. Imagine now sending your breath into those dark or empty patches, or where you can feel the emotion in your body, and watch it dissolve away or disintegrate it.

7. Imagine breathing into your mind, and the thoughts that live there which limit or upset you in some way. Dissolve them away by using the above techniques or taking away their power by pushing them backward with your breath. If that isn't working and the thoughts are still there, use the breath to zoom out the picture so that the feelings and thoughts are tiny, and then explode them with a laser of breath.

You might have noticed I used the term 'dissolve away' when referring to removing upsetting thoughts from your experience in this recipe. When I say this, I'm referring to the use of breath healing in the dissolving process to completely eliminate the thoughts. We want them to totally 'go away'. I'll use this term to work with eliminating pain or anything we no longer want to see in our experience. It's a trigger to the brain to continue dissolving until the depths of the words/issue/pain are completely gone.

We can use the breath in healing to activate the heart intelligence to remove an energy block, a physical symptom, and an upsetting emotion. When you are asked to breathe into the emotion or pain, you imagine that your breath can bypass the limits of your lungs and can be aimed at the required point, almost in the same way you would with a laser beam. This gives you the ability to empower your healing into a deeper level. You can do this to relieve the symptoms of a cramp or headache or other symptoms.

When you've mastered using your breath, you can change any of your limiting behaviour patterns. It just takes practice to get the hang of it. We'll be using breath in all of the healing meditations, and many of the other techniques and recipes in this book too, to help you to make your own transformation.

Meditation: Daily Reset to Spirit

Do this meditation initially every day to fit in best with your schedule. Choose morning, night, or sometime during the day. Read or speak it slowly, with pauses at the end of sentences. Take yourself to a quiet space where you'll not be interrupted for a while. Turn off your phone, close the door and get yourself comfortable.

Close your eyes now.

Taking some nice big deep breaths ... slowly now ... just breathing nice and deep and slow.

You are aware of your body and are aware of the sounds in the room as you breathe.

And as you breathe, you are focusing upon those same sounds until they fade away.

You can just hear my voice now ... everything else has faded into the background.

You are beginning to feel ever so relaxed.

Breathing even deeper, your breathing is becoming slow.

You are becoming even more relaxed.

As you breathe, you bring your focus to the area around your forehead between the eyebrows.

You imagine your breath can breathe here.

Breathe into this space.

As you breathe, you find yourself imagining or becoming aware of a beautiful and brilliant bright white light above you.

You feel it's light and it feels like love ... so warm and so loving.

As you breathe, you see the white light pouring down over you, surrounding you in this love.

This white light pours down through the top of your head and its love permeates everything that is you.

Your body is becoming filled with white light.

Every part of you is illuminated.

Worries and sadness and anger fade away.

You feel yourself breathing deeply ... even more slowly ... and you are so relaxed and feeling ever so happy.

The white light is pouring through you now ... penetrating into the earth below, seeking the centre.

As it reaches the core of the earth, you feel this feeling of safety flooding through every part of you ... and you feel ever so safe.

As you look down, you notice that your heart has become filled with light and that the light seems anchored here.

As you breathe, you notice the light is expanding from your heart outwards with your breath.

You look above and feel reassured by the light and its infinite connection.

You feel the infusion of certainty, of such a faith in the Universe and your place within it.

You just know that everything is going to be okay, no matter what the world throws at you.

Your heart is expanding.

You feel such love and connection with the Universe and with everyone and everything in it.

As you breathe you begin to feel your awareness of the room and its sounds returning.

You feel different, there's a connection here that you hadn't anticipated.

You feel love.

You feel loving and loved, you are ready for the day.

Put your feet on the ground ... feel its strength connecting with you.

Rest in the peace of this energy and connection for as long as you like.

Rise slowly when you are ready, or snuggle down into sleep.

Hawaii, Sacred Healing

W ow.
What a whirlwind. I can't believe that I'm actually sitting on the plane, that I've completed all the tests and scans and prepared everything for the business and our home and animals while we're away.

As we board and settle ourselves into our seats, I find myself in the most surreal of circumstances. I am carrying what still seems to be a huge tumour. Could it possibly be real? Am I dreaming? Has the past week actually happened? As I gingerly press my back into the seat, I feel the pain from the biopsy site and figure that this is actually the real deal. Dreams are over. I'm sitting well and truly in the centre of reality, and it's not such a great place to be. I've been poked and prodded with needles and radiology machines for scans and tests, and I'm definitely feeling tired and sore from it all.

The biopsy was a nightmare. They used a massive needle to access the tumour via my back to minimise damage to my abdominal organs. I can tell you right now that my back muscles do not feel like they've been in any way minimised! The insertion was difficult due to the extreme calcification of the tumour—just as I saw in my meditation—and the pain was excruciating. Alas, as luck would have it, they scraped past a nerve which adhered to the needle causing even more searing pain.

OUCH!

They had to begin again. I was curious to see the samples of the tumour, which were suspended in fluid. I was surprised to feel love rather than disgust or anger. I know my body is trying to communicate with me that it has been, and still is, very toxic.

I'm tired. This has been the most emotionally draining week. It has been so hard to slip into sleep and if I manage that, it's restless and broken sleep. By contrast, I am also very happy and peaceful. It's weird really, a time of extremes, as my great faith is interspersed with times of panic and exhaustion.

I'm not entirely sure what's waiting on the other side of this trip, yet I'm just trying to be in the now. I'm trying to live today and worry about tomorrow later. Fear comes and goes as I breathe deeply into its enormity to dissolve it away.

There are seven of us, including four of our five children and one son's partner, so logistically, it's quite a challenging trip. This is not usually a problem for me, I love a project. I just love planning and I've been working on every detail for months. I want to make it a trip that is the most incredible experience for all involved. Almost every detail has been ticked off. It's such a shame our eldest daughter can't get time off work, but she's not long started a new job.

This trip is so special for our family as it's also Nanna's last gift. My much-loved mother-in-law, Zita, passed away just over three years ago. Bern was determined to share her legacy and inheritance by creating an incredible memory of her generosity. It's a tricky thing to create a legacy for both of us, as well as five children with varied personalities and interests. Especially when their ages span from eight to twenty-seven!

I've spent months pouring over books and travel websites creating the most amazing trip. Four islands in ten days means we're in for an intense, jam-packed itinerary, filled with the most incredible experiences. When I created the itinerary, I felt Zita's gentle guidance toward locations, accommodation and suppliers.

As I sit on the plane, I know with anticipation that her gift is going to help me to heal my cancer.

She's allowing each of us to spend quality time together, and time for each of us to work through our grief and the fear that my diagnosis has stirred. What an incredible gift to give us the opportunity to be in the energies of Hawaii at this time, one of the most healing places in the world. This has the greatest synchronicity for me, as I know it would give Zita such joy to be making a massive difference with her inheritance at this very challenging time. I feel tears of gratitude filling my eyes as I see the day I sat in the hospital some years before, channelling healing into her breast for her own cancer. It is almost like she is here, bringing me her own special healing.

I am very introspective and at times melancholy on the flight. I am seated next to Zavier, who is finding it very difficult to grasp the concept that he is now living on Hawaii time, meaning he should be asleep!

Oh, how I wish he was asleep!

I am *so* tired, and the events and repeated sleeplessness of the last week are adding to my frustration. Berni and I were going to swap seats so that he could look after Zavier after some movies and food, but the guy in the aisle seat next to me took a pill and is fast asleep. There is no passing him, no going anywhere. As Zavier wriggles and tosses and turns, I eventually give up on my own comfort and snuggle him into my chest. Having both of us tired and grumpy will not go well, methinks. Of course, he melts into my chest and sleeps very well.

I, on the other hand, am left alone with my thoughts as sleep refuses to come.

It's such a weird space to be in. I'm feeling fragile, but I think we all are to differing degrees. We're all trying to be brave and okay about it all. I'm hoping the busy itinerary and the awesomeness of the activities planned will melt all that away.

As we transit from Honolulu to the island of Kauai, I am so excited for the opportunity to visit the pristine energies of this beautiful place. I feel like I've been waiting to be here forever: Hawaii feels like a spiritual home.

Our first activities are booked for the next day, where Bern will take Lachy, Dylan and Sian on a downhill bike ride from the top of Waimea Canyon. It's known as the Grand Canyon of the Pacific and it's supposed to be amazing.

Zavier is too young, so Maddie and I head off with him to the other side of the island to go horseriding. After hiring a car and successfully managing my first hour of driving on the wrong side of the road without crashing, we find ourselves in the most incredible ranch amidst the rainforest. We've booked a private ride and the horses are mostly steady, despite the deep mud underfoot. Able to relax on this beautiful animal, I am left to drink in the incredible energy of the ranch as we ride through the beautiful surrounds. I'm super aware of everything I am doing and so sensitive to every feeling right now. It's like I am a highly-tuned instrument. Last week, every movement was a worry, yet here I find myself feeling ever so free, despite the walking pace of our horses. Something inside me adjusts and I'm suddenly feeling so at one with this place. There's a sense of oneness with the land and everything upon it. I feel like I belong here, despite my love for Australia.

Our next activity is kayaking into the rainforest to hike to a sacred pool, and this time, we're all together. There are also a number of other people on the tour here, so it's not exactly private, despite the difficulty in getting there. It doesn't seem to matter. I can feel the pool way before we reach it—it's calling to me.

Now, to be really honest, I've never been a fan of swimming where the water isn't warm. Yet strangely, I feel little reluctance as I stumble over the rocks and into the pool. As I submerge my body in the water, I feel something pop inside and the pain that has been living deep under my conscious awareness for decades just washes away. I stand in the water and take in my surroundings, and make a memory. Which is pretty lucky, because my brand new underwater camera hasn't survived the swim; it's filled with water, so who knows how the photos will turn out!

As we make our way back to the harbour, I find it hard to focus on walking and kayaking when I have so little stamina, so Berni's doing more than his fair share of paddling. For the first time, my fierce independence is gone and I don't even care!

By the afternoon, I am still in a state of euphoria, despite my tiredness, as we board the helicopter to explore the mostly uninhabited island of Kauai. Maddie gets serious motion sickness and it isn't hard to understand why, as we drop into crater shafts and swing in and around the cliffs and mountains.

I am overwhelmed by the healing energy I feel pulsating through every part of my body and energy. I can't explain it, but I feel myself healing. Every second is so amazing, and the energy of our surroundings makes me ultra-aware of the changes I am feeling inside my tumour.

I'm feeling so positive that I think the Universe must be speaking to me, and right at that moment, a rainbow appears directly beside us. As rainbows symbolise abundance and dreams coming true, I'm so excited that I can barely breathe. I would literally reach out and touch it if I could open the window.

In that moment, I know without a doubt that I am going to be okay, and this cancer experience is nothing more than a journey I must travel.

I feel my fear of dying disappear.

After only three days in Kauai, we fly to Maui and I'm already wishing we'd planned to stay longer. The moment I step onto this island, it feels like I've come home! We're staying in a couple of condos close to where our tours leave. Ours has very traditional sixties Hawaiian décor and I'm spooked to find a cockroach! Visions of large cockroaches crawling over me make falling to sleep difficult later that night. I am not an insect fan!

Early the next morning we're off on a tour to snorkel in the healing waters surrounding the island of Maui. I'm not a super fan of swimming in the ocean, it's always scared me to dive into open water. Probably something to do with drowning on the Titanic in a past life, I guess. But I'm trying to live without limits these days, so I carefully lower myself in. Maddie spends the trip unwell again; the poor love is green, and she's refusing to do any more helicopters or boats! I can hardly blame her.

Our next stop is known as the 'Big Island', and is very special in an entirely different way. We are standing on a massive volcano which is literally creating the black rock of the island as we speak, and it's exuding another energy entirely. I feel myself being grounded into the beautiful energies of Hawaii, and my heart opening, as I become one with her heart.

I understand the connection to the land that indigenous peoples experience much better now, as I feel my own connection growing to this sacred part of the Earth. It feels like the islands of Hawaii are alive, and in my becoming still, it has opened my eyes and my heart to the intrinsic character and energy of this place. I know the many islands of Hawaii will be sacred to me forever.

Can this trip get any better?

That evening we find ourselves swimming with the manta rays, despite my fears. What an incredible experience this is turning out to be. We are floating around a light suspended within a surfboard, so they won't be harmed by inadvertently touching us. It's surreal watching them glide underneath our bodies.

I can feel my fear coming in waves, and I suddenly see clearly how my life has been driven by fear. I don't think I've made a single choice that wasn't divined by fear in some way. Whether I'm evaluating unlikely risks, worrying about offending people or worrying about potential disaster, fear has been my constant companion.

No more.

No more do I want to be driven my fear. Its making my life ever so stressful and I spend too much of my time worrying, or trying to prevent stuff happening that will probably never happen. It's draining me of my energy; energy that I'd prefer to use making my life happier.

I begin the process of letting go, so that *I* can be in charge of my destiny.

I'm breaking up with these old patterns of fear. I might not know every step of how to do it yet, but I'm going to be open to finding out. I'm going to master fear and sit in the quietness to divine a new path forward.

I do it, right then and there.

Every day in every way, I choose to let it all go ... to live every day without limits.

I come out of the water lighter, and feeling incredible.

Little did I know that those changes would create an opportunity the next day which would change me forever.

Before we left Australia, I spent hours researching tour operators to fulfil my visions of swimming with the dolphins. In spiritual circles, dolphins are seen as having a wisdom that far surpasses knowledge on Earth. I was keen to swim with the dolphins, but not if it meant harming them. The company I found was the same one that operated the manta ray swim the night before. I felt their credentials and way of operating was honouring the dolphins and manta rays, and that they protected the welfare of these sea creatures better than most other operators.

We had decided when we were booking that the trip was to be memorable in every way, so we booked a private charter. Never would we have imagined this experience would be under the cloud of a cancer diagnosis and that the private charter would end up as one of our greatest choices.

We're on the boat before dawn, as our operator likes to be first out. It's hilarious really, considering I'm not a morning person and still very sleep deprived. My tiredness is amplifying my fear of the ocean, and it's testing last night's determination to live without limits. I take a breath and step off the boat to wait for the dolphins to pass. We are given instructions on keeping the dolphins safe, and are informed by the operator that the dolphins themselves will choose if they wish to interact with us. If not, they'll either swim deeply under or around us. To our delight, they choose to play and swim with us, curious as to our presence in their waters.

On our last dive, I have the most incredible experience. This is one of the most healing of my whole cancer journey.

I am in the water, this time with the guide, who grabs my hand to pull me to a spot in the water. He's a powerful swimmer and he's gone before I notice why I am here. He points and when I follow his finger, I can see three dolphins swimming and jumping in unison in the distance.

My eyes widen as I realise they are swimming toward me!

I don't know if they are swimming slowly, or time slows down, or both! I can feel their voices inside me, imploring me to be at one with them. I don't move, just stare in awe as they move nearer and nearer, until I realise their unison movements are so close and perfect, it's as if they are one.

They swim upwards towards my chest, curving underneath me to dive down at the last second. The dorsal fin of the centre dolphin is millimetres from my heart and I am gently buffeted by a wave of love, as the rippling of water buffets my body. For a moment that seems to last forever, I am at one with the dolphins.

My heart empties its pain and opens bigger than the expanse of the Universe. I feel the intelligence of my heart awakening, as the pain lifts and an extraordinary innate wisdom awakens into my awareness.

Although the waters are clear, visibility becomes even more perfect, as the ocean lights up like a beacon. The guide brings me back to the now, as I notice him waving excitedly. "Did you see that! It doesn't get any closer than that!"

It's taken my breath away, so I can only wave and nod in response. I feel such incredible joy.

After this experience, I feel complete.

My heart has been reawakened from the pain of the past. I know now that I have the capacity and the time to fully heal myself. After driving across the island to go zip lining, I find myself totally at peace. Even Berni's impatience at running late (unusual for him, I can tell you), brushes off me. David has banned me from any activity that could create an impact on the tumour, so zip lining is out for me.

As I wave to the others, I wander into the forest below, along the riverbed. I've got a lot of time to fill, so I take my time, drinking in this very different volcanic energy.

Eventually, I find myself at a pair of trees and am spontaneously drawn to one of them. I'm not usually a tree hugger, so I surprise myself when I throw my arms around the tree. Yet I know there's a purpose, so I close my eyes and breathe.

At once, the tree and I are one, and I can feel it's roots sinking deep into the earth. I feel the pulsating of the earth from within and realise I cannot feel any separation between us. The energy of Hawaii seems to be charged and melded with my own and I feel time disappear. We have become one, and I know now that I can feel this at any time. I am filled with a peace and joy that is bigger than the words of our language.

I realise that no one knows where I am, so I head back to the reception platform just in time to take photos of everyone on their last zip line. I'm so excited that I drop the Tiffany necklace I gave to Berni for Valentine's Day through a crack in the decking. As I am unable to find it, a kind guy who was walking through offers to go underneath the decking to search for it. My experience has been so powerful that even losing his precious necklace, which symbolises the key to my heart, cannot phase me. I feel like the essence of love with every breath I take. It's so beautiful.

It's been such a great day. I'm in this utopia and bliss, as I settle to sleep.

Our final helicopter tour is scheduled just before we fly to Honolulu. Flying over a live volcano and its lava is surreal, you can actually see rock being formed as other rock appears to be destroyed or melted away. It's like nothing ever stays the same and creates a timely reminder for me that everything is and will continue to change. I think of the cells of the body and how they are in a constant state of renewal.

Knowing the body replaces and renews itself constantly, expands my faith in the ability of my body to heal the cancer.

Honolulu is a busy city and makes a stark contrast to the peace and tranquillity of the other islands, yet I'm happy for this experience of shopping, relaxing and eating with those I love. Life just seems too perfect right now and it takes me by surprise to remember that I have cancer, and will need to consider treatment options on my return.

It's not until that evening when the doctor's rooms call to schedule my appointment that I snap out of my euphoria. The tone of her voice means she knows it's as bad as I believe it to be. As Berni continues his nightly ritual of healing me with his hands, accentuated by essential oils, crystals and his love, I remember myself.

I will make it; this is not a bad thing.

The tumour now feels less solid in parts, but it doesn't seem to be much smaller. Berni promises me that WHEN, not IF, I beat this cancer, he will take me on a holiday anywhere in the world to celebrate. As I float in the Waikiki waves in the sunshine on our last day, I am peaceful. I speak to my highest wisdom and to my guardian angel about what I must face in the future. I feel calm and certain, and I know I want to return here to Hawaii. I'm sure our credit card just let out a sigh of relief that it isn't Europe!

༄

Returning to Melbourne is bittersweet. I feel like I am letting go of a well-loved romance and returning to one I'm not so fond of. Not that I dislike David, but let's just say it's not love yet.

As we wait in reception for our appointment to discuss the results, both Berni and I are nervous. I've already told Berni to expect the worst, so it can only get better from there. David ushers us into his spacious office with a serious face and gives us the news I don't want to hear. He speaks to me as a nurse and I take what he says and translate it into language Berni can understand.

The biopsy shows I have a very aggressive and even rarer tumour than the original scans had indicated. Yesterday's scans show it could be marginally smaller but is still contained. The sample is very calcified, like bone, which means analysis was difficult and the diagnosis could revert to the equally serious liposarcoma. Because it's so rare, there is little in the way of good studies to prove the outcomes of treatments. What they do know is that chemotherapy doesn't work on this type of cancer, so radiation is my only medical option to combine with surgery.

He discusses the studies that I am by now very familiar with. He hopes that with radiation therapy I could have a very slight chance of reducing the possibility of recurrence. He frowns when I ask a pointed question.

"If that was true, then why is there no associated drop in the overall mortality of the study groups?" I tell him I've never been a fan of this type of therapy or its side effects. He wants me to discuss it with the top radiation oncologist.

At that next appointment, we discuss the risk of creating more malignant tumours in the healthy tissue which must be killed in the process. It's the only way for the radiation to reach the tumour. She explains it's against the odds, but smiles ruefully when I point out that my odds aren't that great right now with this kind of tumour. I can't see the risk of more malignant cancers later on as an acceptable risk for what is by far a very uncertain and unlikely set of outcomes.

I think David has decided that I'm his worst nightmare. Too questioning, too logical, yet respectful at all times of his knowledge and experience. Challenging the limits of western medicine and forcing him to admit that he can give me no hope or guarantees in anything is not easy for either of us.

Right now, medicine cannot offer me a cure.

He joins us at the end of the appointment with the two other specialist doctors and asks me what I'd like to do.

I think of the time in Hawaii where I experienced no fear, where I knew I would make it, and I knew I would be guided. I thought of the last day swimming in Honolulu and of the angel who appeared to me as I was floating in the ocean. I remembered the total lack of fear in her presence, and the clarity that came from communicating with her, and the peace it brought. I remembered floating in the warmth of the water, and the decision I made in that moment.

"David, I would like to proceed with surgery as soon as possible."

David turns pale, and he's clearly choosing his words carefully as he ponders my response.

I tell him that if I had my way, I'd just take the time to heal the tumour myself as I'd seen in so many others, but my intuition is guiding me towards immediate surgery. He starts pulling out consent forms. "If it's a choice between you going off and doing nothing, or proceeding with surgery alone, then let's get you to surgery."

I feel like I have just stepped onto a rollercoaster that I don't want to ride.

Identifying Your Truth

I remember what it is like to die, the joy of returning home being compromised by the pangs of letting go of those you love here ...

When you die, it's like you wake up from a dream. You find yourself surrounded by familiar souls who have so much love for you, and with whom you share your love. You wake up and everything is so incredibly light and bright, and you are surrounded in every way by this brilliant bright white light that infuses everything. It's bigger than anything you remember of Earth. As you awaken and rest, taking time to adjust to your surroundings, you gather those same souls close to you. You have much to say. You're returning from the most incredible adventure and you feel humbled by the opportunities you've had to learn.

You share adventures and experiences alike, focusing upon the positives and negatives of each aspect of every occurrence. You find that you have the ability to be here and there at the same time, aware of the happenings in your absence on Earth, while engaged in the interactions with these love-filled souls.

Your journey in reading and experiencing the healing created by this book will be similar.

One day you'll wake up, surrounded by supportive and loving souls in human form. You'll be incredulous that you could have been so unhappy, and so unware of just how unhappy you were on the inside (especially with the knowledge of just how happy you will become). You'll laugh at just how little you knew of the brilliance that is you. You'll feel sad at how many years you wasted feeling limited, frustrated, negative, self-critical, judgemental—especially when you think of today. Today was the day you began to change. You put it in your calendar, knowing it would be important later on.

Self-love isn't something we're raised to focus upon. Even children with the most supportive, loving and encouraging of parents can find themselves frustrated with their own sense of inadequacy.

Each of us has at least one mentor as we grow; perhaps for you it's a parent, sibling, relative, teacher, neighbour or friend. They make a difference, reminding you that not all is as bad as we might believe. Yet despite their best efforts, you go out into the world of school, of work, of playgrounds and parks to be among people. These people don't really care about nurturing your feelings of goodness about yourself. They're busy trying to cope in a world that's just as challenging and at times overwhelming for them as it is for you. They're distracted and at times insensitive to what's happening in your life.

Regardless of how good-hearted a person is, they are likely to be hurtful at some stage to someone's feelings, or break another's heart. Sometimes it's intentional, but more often than not, it isn't. They're just not thinking, or they don't realise the impact of their actions, as it's totally outside their awareness and/or experience.

They move on in life, surrounded by their own thoughts of coping and inadequacy. You get left with a feeling you don't like, and you try to make it fit into some form of common sense.

Sometimes it's like you're writing a story. There are so many possible endings and you choose the one that fits with what you know at the time. But what if that story was wrong? What if you ended up not liking what you saw in yourself for all the wrong reasons? Life could turn a paler shade of brilliant, and while you might feel like you're happy, it's because you don't know just how good it can get.

My first marriage was like that. I was old enough at twenty-four to assume that I knew what I wanted. It was simple.

I wanted security and someone to love me.

I wanted a peaceful home where children weren't smacked for discipline and didn't have to grow among the fights and arguments of their parents. I wanted someone who would adore my children and prioritise them over everyone and everything. I wanted someone who would see a woman as important.

I thought that I had found that.

Despite him insisting we needed to live together first to ensure he was making the right choices, I believed he would love me enough to create the happily ever after. His reason for 'living in sin' as it was known then, was that he hated watching how much his mother was hurt by the actions of his father.

Okay, I thought, this guy looks like he honours a woman.

Tick!

We'd talked about children, and he seemed fine with disciplining through love and teaching rather than physical punishment.

Tick!

He was keen to have two children and agreed that 'the more kids the less time', so two was looking good.

Tick!

He said he loved me.

Tick!

I guess he's the one ...

How do you know when you have the one? Was I even in a position to be choosy? I was pretty enough, but I had crooked teeth, wore glasses and had thin hair that would become oily without daily washing. Not to mention the whole psychic visions thing. I was not exactly what I would call a great catch.

However, I couldn't see that I was fun, that I laughed a lot and made other people laugh too. I couldn't see the value of my kindness. I couldn't see how massive my capacity to love others was, and that being loved by me made people happy. I couldn't see how valuable my high level of caring and support for people was. I couldn't see that I might be beautiful or sexy.

Those men had wrecked that ...

When I was ten years old, I had an experience that haunted my dreams for the following twenty years. I would wake in terror, picturing myself on an entry porch with four other children of similar ages to me. I'm frightened and they're all watching me with expressions I don't understand. They're confused and angry and worried and scared all at the same time. I can hear a woman's voice.

"What the hell did you have to go and do that for? Drunk again, you can't even control yourself when you're sober. Now what do you expect me to do? What am I going to tell her mother?"

There follows mumbling, and then she raises her voice again. "Oh, great idea that. Her father will kill you and end up in jail, and then there'll be two families without fathers to feed them!"

The dream is always the same: same place, same faces and same words. I wish I understood their meaning, but at the same time, I know that I don't want to know.

My mother trusted the shouting woman enough to allow me to stay the night. I was to have a sleepover for two nights; a weekend away from home. I was returned the next morning. She claimed I was homesick and crying too much and glared at me to defy her. My eyes were swollen and red. There was nothing to indicate she was lying, because she wasn't.

I needed to be home so desperately that I was unable to speak, as during the night before, my sense of safety in the world was pulled out from under me, and now my parents were being robbed of the ability to protect me.

I said nothing and slunk away from my mother's disapproving eyes to sneak my pants into the washing machine. As I watched them sink into the sudsy water, I saw the drops of blood on them blur like tears.

My mother wasn't to know that I'd woken in the night, unable to breathe due to the enormous weight that was squashing my body. That the woman's husband was on top of me in his daughter's bed. I had been too shy to share with her sister, so she had generously offered to swap and give me her bed.

My legs were forced apart and my pants were missing. There was searing pain between my legs ...

My terror cannot be described in words. I'd never been exposed to anything like this in my life, neither the assault or the resulting action. I did not know what was happening to me and so I acted instinctively. I screamed, or did I call out? He responded by clamping his big hand over my mouth, inadvertently blocking my nose at the same time.

Now I really couldn't breathe and the pain was intensifying in my 'mini', as I referred to my vagina. I struggled and managed to bite him as hard as I could. He yelled out in shock and then the lights were on. The woman was standing there and grabbed him, dragging him from the room.

I don't remember her returning, or even replacing my pants, although I imagine she must have, as I was once again wearing them in the morning. I was in shock and couldn't get the smell of drinking out of my nostrils. It had a weird, foreign smell that was burning my nostrils. I lay in the bed so still, too petrified to move, waiting for him to come back.

I was quiet in the morning and couldn't stop crying.

I just wanted my mum.

Mum was cross with me for a couple of days, figuring I was being a baby about things, lacking confidence, and unable to handle a simple sleepover with a trusted family.

Her words describing what she perceived as my 'lack' sank into me and became my truth due to the trauma I was experiencing.

I was impatient with myself for every day that I didn't tell her, until the day came when I couldn't say anything about it at all.

I figured that her attempts at jollying me into feeling more confident were statements of fact. I assumed her words meant she knew what was wrong with me and why it had happened; after all, she was my mum. I sounded like a terrible little girl and that was obviously why he tried to hurt me. I would look at myself with such irritation and realised I must have deserved it. I would have to work harder at being good.

A couple of months later, Nanny had us over to stay to give Mum a break. She ended up taking us to the doctor as my sister had a sore bottom and I had a sore 'mini'. It turned out my sister needed medicine, but the doctor and Nanny had to chase me around the room for the examination. I was too terrified to let him see or touch me there, even though the pain was unbearable. I believed it was my punishment.

As he wrote a prescription for a cream, he looked at Nanny, who he had known for years, and asked her if everything was okay at home. Was someone hurting me? She looked horrified and said of course not. I couldn't speak a word. He suggested that she might be wise to keep a closer eye on things.

Upon our return to her home, she asked me point blank. I couldn't answer as she looked me in the eyes. "Did someone hurt you at your house?"

I shook my head, and she looked relieved. I can't imagine how hard it must have been for her to even contemplate that something bad was happening under her son's roof.

"Did someone hurt you at school?"

Again, I shook my head. Confused, she said she'd need to talk to my parents about this. I was so scared that I started crying hysterically. "No! No! No! I'll get in more trouble, please don't tell anyone anything!" She reluctantly agreed and I promised I'd tell her if anyone hurt me.

A year or so later, another trusted male in the large group surrounding my family would begin a series of betrayals of the trust placed in him.

He told me that I was just so beautiful and that it wasn't his fault that he needed to love me like that ...

He said it every time he did bad things to me. I knew they were bad, as he was always furtively checking as to who was around. He had always said we couldn't tell anyone, and that we'd both get in trouble.

Telling Mum was also complicated by the fear of Dad going to jail. It didn't stop until I remembered something I'd heard someone else say.

"Stop it! I'll tell my dad, and he'll ... and he'll kill you with his gun!" I was so surprised at those words, and even as they came out, I was shocked at the strength and anger behind them, but the damage had already been done.

It had to be true. Bad things happen to beautiful girls. So, I couldn't be beautiful anymore. I would hide away my body and budding breasts as they grew. My pelvis would turn inward and my bottom outward to hide my 'mini'. My shoulders rounded to hide away that which made me a girl. I didn't have anyone to argue with me as I told no one. While I didn't understand why Dad might shoot either of the men with a gun, I couldn't take the risk that two families of children would be starving. If I couldn't tell them what happened the last time, then I couldn't take the risk that Dad would end up in jail by telling them this time.

I was too young at that time to really understand that what had happened to me was due to the bad behaviour of those men. I mistakenly believed that I was at fault, that I was naughty and beautiful which had made the bad things happen. I withdrew into myself and my shyness, something that I would struggle with until cancer raised its head.

I lost my belief in myself and the ability to see myself through my own eyes. Not long after, I would need glasses, compounding my already growing feelings of being unacceptable. I began to self-evaluate millions of times throughout the course of a day. I was so harsh in my criticisms if I found myself to be lacking. Before long, this had become a pattern of behaviour that was a part of me. So much a part of me that I couldn't recognise when I was being cruel or impatient with myself.

It would take over twenty years for me to sleep a whole night through, before I remembered the entire experience and sought healing and counselling. A whole part of my life came back to me.

Self-love is about recognising that which makes you intrinsically beautiful. It isn't about your looks or size or skin colour or origins or religion. It's an inner magic, a beauty that can be discerned from the outside. One that acts like a magnet which draws others to your light.

It's confidence, yet it's more.

It's intelligence, yet it's innate in us all.

It's beauty, yet it's nothing that can be seen with the eyes.

It's an irresistible magic, yet not one that you have to create.

Self-love stems from the heart intelligence and permeates throughout everything. It creates an open heart, one that gives and most importantly, receives. That heart and its love is pointed inward, directly to the heart self. It thrives on the acknowledgment of everything that makes you brilliant and feeds on being nurtured by you with kindness, support and love.

It's pretty hard to feed and nurture and love yourself if you're not in a great space. You feel too flat to even know when you're not loving yourself. If we don't know what's possible, we'll settle for what we've got.

I settled in my first marriage by marrying him in the first place. I married him not because I was madly in love with him, but because he felt safe. He seemed like a 'good' man, but as time went on it became very clear that he was not 'my man'.

I was so desperate for love that I convinced myself that I really loved him. I certainly loved being loved by him, but I know now that this feeling was not the kind of love that would sustain me in future years.

By the time we were finally engaged, I knew he didn't really love me either, not in the way I needed to be loved. I needed to be heard, and to be told of his love, which didn't happen. His constant tormenting and teasing at my expense would only contribute to my seriously low opinion of myself.

I gave myself away little bit by little bit.

Every time there was an argument over what he believed to be 'lacking' in my personality or behaviour, I began to believe him. After all, it didn't seem that far from what I already knew. I tried so hard to please him but it was never enough.

Soon, all the things he loved or liked about me had become casualties of our arguments and our relationship was doomed. Of course, it would take a further ten years of damage to finally push me into valuing and choosing me by walking away from the marriage.

Action!
Living in the Moment

One of the tools which has made the most difference over the past twenty years has been learning to live in the moment. Although in saying that, it was one of the hardest things to maintain as I was progressing through my cancer journey. Our fear naturally wants to alarm us, that's why the ego uses it, to help us to know that a change in your choices, behaviours or attitude is warranted or needed. What is meant to happen is that when fear arises, we go into our stillness to allow the intuitive part of us to guide the way to an easier path filled with joy.

Most of us miss that second part, as we get caught up in the drama or worry of the situation. It's hard not too, as our past experiences of difficulty and drama come to mind. Yet, if you can master living in the moment, you can literally take the joy from every day, and life just keeps on getting better.

That's what is important. If you are living in the moment, the only thing that matters is now, not tomorrow or your to-do list or the dramas of the day. Living in the moment will create the ability to make every moment a potential feeder of joy. The happier you are, the happier the people will be who are around you, the happier your experience, and the less likely you are to stress over the little things.

Living in the moment actually detaches you from fear and worry, and I've found an easy way to do that—using the power of gratitude.

If you live in the moment, you are so aware of all that is good or great or fabulous in your life. The more you focus upon it, the happier you get. The happier you are, the more you notice how good things are, and you feel hopeful and excited about what can happen in the future. So, in this moment, I'm grateful for my comfy chair and desk, my computer with its ergonomic keyboard, the heater on this chilly day, the view of the pool and foliage from the window, the opportunity to do something creative, the cup of tea that was just made for me, and the delicious lunch that's being prepared for me. I'm grateful that I have a roof over my head, nice and comfy clothes to wear, and the bathroom I'm about to visit. I'm also grateful that the girls are managing the running of Flying Souls and our projects so that I can do what I love, and that's writing for you.

If I focus on everything that is good or fuelling me in this moment, then what we focus upon actually grows. The negative falls away or loses its importance or intensity.

I feel more capable and because I'm grateful for everything I have in the moment, and my heart is opening and my energy is drawing more of the same to me. I am a magnet for my experience, and knowing that focusing upon good or bad will amplify either, I'm focused upon amplifying the good rather than the bad. I'm hardly interested in feeding anything bad in my life, so the good it is.

When I live in the moment, I'm more aware of the yearnings of my body, mind and spirit. Because I'm happier, I'm enthusiastic about making possibilities grow and I find I'm treating myself better. If I need food or sleep or exercise or water or love or stimulation or rest or meditation, I'll try to make that happen.

As I work more on living in the moment, I'll be doing more of what's needed. I'm getting happier and more fulfilled by the moment.

When you're living in the moment, you can see how important it is to have moments of stillness. Stillness allows us the space to make less emotionally reactive choices or decisions, and allows us the ability to access our intuitive wisdom.

Here's my recipe for connecting and going into the stillness inside to make it even easier to access our inner wisdom.

Accessing the Stillness

1. Find a quiet spot where you won't be interrupted.

2. Using what you know already about breath, fill your body with joy and dissolve away any negative feeling or emotions or discomfort in your body.

3. Focus upon imagining that you can breathe further than the limits of your lungs and breathe into your heart.

4. As you breathe into your heart, imagine it growing and becoming bigger and bigger.

5. As your heart grows, you feel yourself becoming quiet and still, you feel a sense of love through everything.

6. Your mind is quieting with every breath you take.

7. Your heart is the keeper of your greatest wisdom. Sit in this space and watch for signs or feelings, or listen for words which show you your next step. All of the guidance will feel like love, or be positive and kind in its approach. If it's not, breathe even deeper and wait for the guidance that awaits you, for that's the voice of your highest wisdom.

8. Try not to 'try' or force the answers, just be patient and sit in the stillness until they come to you.

The more time I spend connecting to my stillness, focusing upon moments as they occur, the more I will be able to take from or create the joy in those moments. I'm more spontaneous, I'm happier and a lot less stressed. Life just keeps on getting better.

Meditation: Heart Healing

Do this meditation every day for seven days, then at least once a week.

Read or speak it slowly, with pauses at the end of sentences. Take yourself to a quiet space where you'll not be interrupted for a while. Turn off your phone, close the door and get yourself comfortable.

It's time to breathe ... to let go.

To allow your heart to heal.

As you breathe, you are slowing each breath ... in through the nose ... out through the mouth.

Every breath is making you more and more relaxed.

As you breathe, you feel your breath almost passing through the confines of your lungs.

It's almost as if you can breathe anywhere in the body.

Breathing slower and slower ... your body knows now that it is safe.

Each and every breath makes you feel even safer.

As you breathe, you find your breath is naturally going into the heart.

Your heart responds with such joy and peace with each and every breath.

You can feel your internal intelligence and wisdom being awakened as your body is dropping into peace.

Your body is feeling ever so safe and relaxed.

Every muscle is softening as you give it your attention.

Your legs.

Your arms.

Your abdomen.

And back.

Your neck and head.

As you breathe deeper and deeper, you watch the breath softening the chest and it is now that you are becoming aware of the tightness there.

The area around your heart feels restricted in some way.

Or tight.

Or perhaps painful.

You might even notice a darkness around the area of your heart.

You focus upon breathing ever so slowly.

Indicating to your body that you are ever so safe.

As you breathe, you feel your awareness moving to the tightness or pain within the heart.

You get the sense that you are surrounded by healing emerald green energy.

That the room has filled with your angels, spirit guides and high-level healers.

It feels warmer somehow and there is such a feeling of love around you.

You give yourself permission to release all that no longer serves you.

And you choose to release it all now.

Waves of fear move in and around you, yet you find yourself strangely comforted as your breath disintegrates them into nothing.

As the fear fades or lessens, you can feel yourself preparing to let go of an old pain, which has haunted your insides for perhaps weeks, years, or even decades.

You feel as if there is a shield protecting the top half of your heart.

Imagining you have spiritual hands, or alternatively using your actual hands, you imagine taking this shield away as if it was real.

Surprisingly, it is not attached to anything, having long outlived its usefulness.

Your heart springs in reaction and expands out large.

You can feel it extending outside the heart cavity.

The heart pulsates with the most powerful energy and you realise you have underestimated its resilience.

You feel such love coursing through your body with each and every beat.

As you breathe deeper and slower, the heart remembers its brilliance and its stretches into every cell it reaches within your body.

Every part of you is beginning to tingle and warm.

Bubbles of joy surprise you, for you had worried healing the heart would be painful.

You see the pain within your heart and you get a sense of who it relates to, perhaps someone who hurt you.

Perhaps someone who left you.

You feel the old emotions of hurt.

Betrayal.

Anger.

Grief.

Anxiety.

Worry.

Fear.

They are now lifting from your heart.

You're not exactly sure why or how.

You look around you to see if you are being healed by the spirit helpers in the room.

You are surrounded by healing.

And while you are receiving healing in this way, this is not the only source of the release inside you.

You are perplexed, but as you watch or feel or imagine, you see that in removing the shield around the heart has awakened it into incredible intelligence.

Your heart and its intelligence are healing you in such a way and with such a speed that no one else could master.

For no one else has walked this path with you, felt the pain and disappointment within you.

No one else knows how you put the pain inside, yet the heart was there.

The heart gathered your pain to release you from it.

Yet you doubted its ability to prevent you from feeling it again.

So, you closed down.

You shut it away and pushed it away or into your body.

But the heart is awake now, and you are now free to clear away the pain, any time you wish.

You feel such joy at the thought of washing away the years of tears and fear.

You feel your heart opening from the inside, releasing the memory that holds the key to your pain.

Despite returning to this painful time.

And it does feel like you're there again, you're feeling strangely detached.

It's like you have taken a different angle in which to see.

Like you're seeing it for the first time.

The pain has no power over you.

And you couldn't be more surprised.

You see the people who were involved in hurting you and you're seeing it from their perspective.

You realise you did not have all the information.

That you assumed things you didn't know.

That there were other things at stake here for them, that had you known ... it may have been different.

You feel your heart opening to them as you remember the good in them ... as you see their light.

You're feeling lighter and freer and your pain is literally melting away.

You know that forgiving the person or persons does not make their behaviour okay, exactly the opposite, for it has brought you pain.

Yet at the same time you know the only person that is suffering from you not forgiving that time, or that situation is you.

You breathe deeply ... allowing the heart healing to pulsate stronger and stronger throughout your body.

You forgive them because you're choosing your happiness and not one of those people deserves or has the right to carry the key to your happiness.

You whisper or say out loud:

"I forgive you all for not being or behaving in the way I needed at that moment ... I forgive you for being unable to support and love me in a way that honoured my soul."

Great waves of love pour through you and you feel such healing and happiness.

But then you are taken aback by a sharp pain through the centre of the heart.

You wonder who you have missed, yet all of the people involved have faded away.

The only person you can see is a lone figure.

That lone figure is you.

You have been carrying the pain of blame.

Perhaps there is pain elsewhere in the body now.

You see that you believe that regardless of the behaviour of others, that you were to blame, and have shouldered it all.

You can see the isolation that came from keeping it hidden.

You know in this moment that you have reached the most important part.

You need to forgive yourself for letting you down.

This was not your fault.

Your actions did not ask for you to be treated in this way.

As you breathe deeply, you whisper:

"I forgive myself for not being or behaving in the way I needed at this moment …

I forgive myself for being unable to support and love myself in a way that honoured me."

Your heart opens widely in response and you feel the pain being extinguished in your body.

You feel such peace and such love coursing throughout your body.

You are becoming aware of your surroundings again and the noises around you.

You take a moment to feel all of the feelings of love, safety and forgiveness and anchor them into your physical body.

You connect your feet to the floor and feel the power of the Earth that lies somewhere beneath you.

You feel it coursing through your body, holding your soul in your body ready for the days ahead.

Breathing deeply, you open your eyes and drink a glass of water.

Taking your time, you arise and return to your day or settle down for sleep.

The Struggle Between Fear & Faith

As soon as we return from Hawaii, it becomes abundantly clear just how much fear was driving my existence, and that I was facing an intensive period of healing and change. What better way of doing it than taking the challenging journey of surgery and everything that will come with that?

As we return from the doctor's surgery, we begin to tell people an edited version of what we know. I tell them that the biopsy shows a cancer that is rarer than the initial diagnosis. That this is very serious and the tumour has become very hard, like bone, and that we've decided to proceed immediately to surgery. Due to the size of the tumour it may take multiple surgeons to work on excising it and any other organs affected. At this stage, I am likely to be at risk of losing my kidney, spleen, and some of my intestine, which could result in a colostomy bag for at least six months. Despite the dire situation of my diagnosis, everyone seems very relieved, and mostly pleased, that the tumour is operable and I'm choosing to have the surgery.

It's really interesting watching people's responses and it gives me a much greater insight into their fears. The idea of me having one of the top surgeons in the country for this type of cancer makes them feel better. Well, not 'better' exactly, but less worried. It allays their fears. As a nurse who's done more colorectal nursing than she cares to remember, it is only marginally comforting. This surgery is massive; it'll take up to ten hours and there's a risk I won't get up off the table alive. And that's before I even begin to think about all the potential complications and what could happen long term. Still, I've got every chance of success and that's why I've chosen David.

Watching their fear is somewhat of a distraction.

Ninety percent of the time, I am travelling along pretty well, organising things and being incredibly positive for the situation I find myself in. Everyone is constantly remarking how incredible I am, that my positivity is so amazing. We all agree that I am coping well. In fact, mostly everyone we've told responds very well to the positive framing of the terrible details, just as we'd hoped. Maintaining a positive energy space around me is essential to how I heal and how I can recover. I've always said that everything is in the presentation, and considering what we're dealing with, we're all, as a collective, going pretty well. Well, we're mostly well, as there are some notable exceptions of people who are losing it, although they are mostly doing it in private.

Ninety percent of the time I am great, but that leaves ten percent and that ten percent is very, very dark. It's in the quiet times, the evenings, or when someone has been upset. It's when the collective numbers of 'the look' start to add up to being unbearable.

'The look' is the face people have when they first see me after they know of my diagnosis. Cancer carries with it a dark cloud. To try to keep it together and to stay positive in front of that face is almost impossible. It comes with compassion, but it also speaks of someone trying to hold it together through their own fears for me and my children. When I see it, I see their fear of my death, and it is beyond confronting. I know it speaks of their care for me, but they have no idea how hard it is to stay positive and to believe in what I know inside, especially when I see it over and over again.

I'm already terrified.

When I'm quiet in bed or sitting on the couch waiting for Berni to bring a tray of tea (one of our routines for connection in our marriage for many years), and I feel his love … that's when I lose it.

The disadvantage of having both an active imagination and repeated exposure to so many incredibly sad and tragic events through nursing and healing, is that it's not hard to step into disaster mode. I can take myself anywhere in my mind in an instant; to my death or to my recovery, as easily as I can take myself into a future with or without me.

When I'm quiet, the fear speaks, and as my story has shown, I've always avoided fear, locking it inside me so I can't feel its pain. I know that as soon as I acknowledge the pain and the fear that is at its core, healing can begin. It is reassuring to know that this process has already begun.

Yet in these dark times, the intensity and enormity of the fear is overwhelming. I don't know what's worse; seeing Berni's love or seeing his fear or tears. They trigger me equally in very different ways.

When I feel his love, my heart breaks for the joy of being loved by him, and the knowledge that soon I might not be here. That this cancer may kill me. It's not what I believe, but it is what my fear screams at me. Never have I been so aware of how fear has managed to take over my way of living.

I can see the times I've engaged in endless planning to avoid mishaps, people getting lost, hurt or disadvantaged. I've always trying to create the perfect outcome for everyone. I see how I've avoided risk, and remember teaching my children risk assessment and problem solving from the age of three. I see myself thinking twice about opening up to people around me, and feeling the pain of peoples' past, so I keep them at arm's length to protect myself. I see myself doing endless hours of research for any new major purchase or trip to protect us from issues. I see myself pouring my love into my children in case I die, so that they may remember me for the love.

In the dark times, I see imaginary glimpses into the future. Sometimes I'm in it and other times not. I see visions of Maddie being pregnant and having questions, but I'm not there to answer them. I see grandchildren born and wistful yearnings from my children for me to be there to know them. I see weddings without me in the front pew, I see graduations without me clapping way too much with embarrassing over-enthusiasm and pride. I see sports carnivals for Zavier and I'm not in the crowd screaming encouragement, I see his school formal (so gorgeous in his suit and tie), and I see his first break-up with a girl without me there to cuddle him better.

I see illnesses in hospital where they can't see my spirit presence, and then them dying, and the joy of being on the other side to greet them. I see family dinners and Christmas lunches. Putting up the Christmas tree is never the same without my enthusiasm for family and celebrating the moment together.

I guess that's it really. A million moments that I will never see from my body ...

Then I shake myself.

I remind myself that I will make it, that this cancer is not a death sentence ... it will not kill me.

Yet I can't help it in these dark times. The fear just takes over ...

I see a vision of Berni lying in bed at night, wracked with tears after having been brave for everyone all day. I feel his deep loneliness and longing for me, his greatest love. He's lost as I see him wandering around the house, touching everything that I've touched, everything I created to surround us with beauty and art and nature. I see him holding my clothes, struggling to do anything with them, let alone boxing them up to give away. I see tears running down his face at the table for all the meals that I'm missing in my chair. I see him holding the children as his tears run with theirs. I see their pain at me being gone and I begin to imagine how I could make it better. Perhaps I could make videos for each of them for the pivotal moments in their lives?

Then I catch myself and remind myself that I will make it, this cancer is not a death sentence ... it will not kill me.

If there's something I do know from over fourteen years of

healing, it's that you have to feel your pain. If you feel your fear and sadness and breathe deeply into it, it can go. I know that as much as it pains me, I must let fear have its way with me. I must allow myself to feel it in its enormity, for it is the *fearing of fear* that makes it so painful. If you allow yourself to feel it in its enormity, it will dissolve. You will be free of it.

So, I allow myself to feel it. I allow myself to acknowledge that I am afraid to die and for all that it will leave behind.

The tears flow and it takes my breath away. I think of Zavier. He is only nine and loves nothing more than cuddles. I see how much he hated Berni and I being away in Paris to renew our vows for a couple of weeks. How will he cope without me? It's not fair that he will grow up without a mum, that he'll live without me.

I think of Lachy who is in his final year of school, under a constant deluge of exams and pressure and deadlines. What effect will my illness have on his results? There's no way you can be focused when you know your mother might die. He too loves cuddles. What if I cannot cuddle him again? How will he be without them or our chats or my healing? The tears are running so thick and fast that I can't see through them anymore.

I think of Maddie who is only twenty and at the beginning of her life. I want to be with her for all the magic and very ordinary moments. What if she can't call to go shopping or for lunch or for anything?

I think of Dylan whose heart is so big and hurts for so many people. What if I can't be there to support and love him in the way I have for so long now? My heart is hurting at the anger and injustice he'll feel at everything for me leaving, and for the pain everyone will experience.

I think of Elyse who is always busy travelling to impoverished countries to help those in need. I love hearing her stories and seeing the myriad of pictures from her travels. What if I'm not there to wonder where she is and if she's safe and what she's doing? How will her life change?

What will it be like for all of them to grow their lives without me? Will they cope? Will they forget me? Will I have mattered? Will they remember me for my love?

I can't see at all anymore, and the tears are now running out of my nose to match the stream from my eyes.

I can feel Berni's love and the warmth of his body as he wraps me in his arms. How did I get so lucky to find this great man and be the centre of his love? What greatness did I do to deserve him? He has always had this ability to hold me tight when things are too big for me. I feel his love, and I borrow his strength until I can find my own. When the world stops spinning, I feel my strength and courage once again coursing through my body, and I can let him and his strength go. He is my rock. I don't know how I could face this without him. He is there for every wave of terror and holds me and heals me until it is gone.

Then I shake myself and remind myself that I will make it, this cancer is not a death sentence ... it will not kill me.

I have my family and friends who are all loving me and hoping for the best and sending as much good vibes and energy as they can. I've allowed them only one of those 'looks', and asked them to try to be as positive as possible. They know that every little bit of their positive energy and love will help make a difference.

I feel stronger now. Fear has had its way with me, I have faced the worst of it and I have survived.

Now to survive the surgery.

Too Hard to Be Me

When I shut down my intuition in response to the death of Nanny, I shut down my ability to discern the easy way through life and became very depressed. I shut down my ability to sit in stillness to access my highest wisdom, and became indecisive and unsure. I removed my internal radar's ability to perceive danger and thus became anxious and on high alert all the time. It was exhausting! I blocked the signals of my internal GPS and things started to get harder and opportunities fell away as I lost my ability to avoid the pitfalls of life.

Being indecisive and unsure got old very quickly and I was so frustrated that I couldn't seem to make up my mind and relied on others to help me decide. In time, my indecisiveness meant my power was also slipping away. I found myself being manipulated into doing things I didn't want to do and hating every moment of it.

I felt happier as I didn't want to see the bad stuff anymore, but I was heartbroken in my grief. My soul was not happy and did everything it could to get my attention. It kept giving me signals and help to get me back on track. I literally had help appearing in front of me without looking for it. Supportive new friends with an interest in the alternative, a reiki healer who taught meditation classes, a tarot reading course, a massage therapist with hands that could heal, books actually falling out of shelves in bookshops, a song with a message, or someone making a random comment that answered my questions. There was no doubt I wasn't on my own and help was there.

Still, my ability had not fully closed down, rather, it waned slightly. When I was talking to a friend in the street, her neighbour's father drove up and walked past us. I saw a vision of him sexually abusing my neighbour's daughter. I became as pale as a ghost and could barely breathe. I blurted out that she was never to allow her daughter to visit when that man was there. A couple of years later his face was plastered all over the news as he was identified as one of Melbourne's worst paedophiles. Fortunately, her daughter was never exposed to his behaviour and the disaster was averted.

Eventually, I gave up resisting and began to reawaken my gifts as I watched my intuitive children grow. I didn't want to be the mum who couldn't help or answer her kids' questions. When I began reiki healings and meditation with Danni, I had a rapid awakening as my gifts came back with a thud. One minute not much was happening, and then the next minute it was like they'd never left me.

I realised that my ability had not decreased in my nursing, as I had been seeing things in the energy of people's bodies the whole time. I had the analgesia for them in my hands as I answered their call bell to complain of pain. I was there with the resuscitation trolley anticipating my patient's last breath as they suffered a heart attack, enabling their successful and full recovery. I knew just what the families of a terminal patient had to say to enable the peaceful passing of their loved one. When I removed my hands from someone in pain, they'd grab my hand and put it back. "Don't take your hand away, you're taking away my pain."

It was Oprah Winfrey and a little boy called Luke who changed my destiny and turned me to the path of healing, and that of teaching others to find happiness, health and wellbeing in their lives.

I awoke before dawn one morning, shaking after another of my terrible 'dreams' where I saw my good friend's little boy in a hospital bed, deathly sick as his family prayed over their rosary beads for him. I rang her and said I'd had a bad dream that he was sick, and could she take him to the doctor. The doctor said he had a virus and sent him home with paracetamol.

That night my dream was more detailed and much worse. I rang in the morning, asking her to take him to the private hospital where I worked, which had a paediatric emergency department. I insisted on paying the fees to ensure she went. Three hours after his admission, they were on the way to the specialist children's hospital to begin chemotherapy. Little Luke, at the age of three, had leukaemia. I was heartbroken.

I was now faced with the dilemma of whether to 'come out' with my gifts or not. I felt that my gifts were part of my destiny and I felt an internal yearning to work with them. Society was not a fan of who I was and I had no idea as to whether I would have a single friend left. My then husband was not a fan either so I was severely compromised at the thought that my children would be ostracised for who I was. But I felt without doubt that I did not have a choice. After what had happened to Luke, I was haunted by the idea of what would have happened if I had chosen to avoid telling his mum. The idea that he could had died because of my cowardice gave me strength.

I looked for mentors and role models of how to go about it.

At the time, Oprah Winfrey was one of the biggest names in the world. Being a black woman on television, she stood up to enormous criticism and negative judgement every day. She believed that she was there to serve and so she did.

I wanted to ask her if she was afraid of the fallout like I was, if she cared what others thought. But I thought of the impact she had made, as I watched her during my years of depression. She made a difference, she gave me hope and she helped me to be brave. Here she was doing it again. I love her for the courage she gave me while I was still looking for my own.

So, I did it. With Luke making a full recovery, I knew that I had this ability for a reason and I chose to be brave enough to give it a go. I meditated, enrolled in healing training and started telling people.

And no one cared. Well, one friend's husband did, but otherwise, everyone embraced me for my ability and so did my family.

It was like I'd been given my life back. Every day just seemed happier!

Action!
The Key to Success

The greatest thing about healing is that it gives you awareness. When you can see just what you're doing and feeling with a sense of objectivity, you have the opportunity to be in charge of your destiny. We all yearn for success, yet it isn't possible to be truly successful if you aren't creating, embracing, taking or pursuing opportunities. So, mastering your fear is important, yet to be truly successful you must master the ability to encourage and support yourself along the way. Looking at the way you see yourself and learning how to manage that is just as important.

So, you cannot be truly successful in all areas of your life if you don't like who you are and what you do. Most of us fail to learn this until we're thick with experience, loss and trauma, as we feel the years of old age creeping up on us.

Imagine if you were to do it now; actually like, approve and applaud your potential. I sometimes sit back and imagine a life like that, and the journey through the big challenges life has given to me. Retrospect is a wonderful thing, isn't it? But what if we could change the concept of retrospect and turn it into something we can learn in the now? Imagine the peace we could experience in our twilight years. Now that would be priceless!

I hope that is what this book is showing. The trauma of my journey through cancer and the insight and clarity it brings, and the events that brought me to that point. I know that my fear of life and the way I interacted with other people has contributed to my body reacting with a tumour. My childhood habits of repressing my emotions and the pain they caused created an acidity in my body. I'm sure my body was so internally inflamed from constantly living in the fear and flight mode of being that it had no choice but to give me a wake-up call. Our bodies aren't made to live like this in the long term. It needed to change straight away. Yet how many of us live like this in some way?

If I can prevent even one person from living a life that isn't full of happiness, I will have achieved my goal.

And you know what? I am so happy now! Why? Because it gave me my life back. Not the one I'd been living, but one that fuels my body and allows my heart to sing. I've just watched my son open his birthday gifts and I'm in such a great place to celebrate with him.

Cancer has been a gift, although I've hated it all the way through! That gift gave me the clarity and drive to stand up and heal this lack of self-love in others. It took me eight months of watching how I was healing people in person to work out how to empower them to do it themselves.

It occurred to me that I needed to create simple, practical and easy ways to give you the clarity and insight to empower yourself. The guided meditations that come with this book have the healing embedded within them. Every chapter has purpose, every word placed in such a way as to allow healing. I've worked out the keys to success, and they're here, ready for you to take charge of your destiny!

You began to heal the moment you picked up this book.

As you've seen with my story, the most important thing is to let go of fear.

It's something that everyone can relate to; we've all suffered from fear. Some of us live more fear than others, but it's not the amount of fear that matters, it's how the fear is driving us.

We're going to start by choosing to **never again** compare ourselves to another. They are who they are, and they are doing the best they can to get through their life. They are not you. They have not had your life experience or influences or background or nurturing or lack of it. They are not you. Their opinions are their own and what they think is none of your business. You can only be accountable for yourself and the journey you are walking. Even those of us who are raising children are simply caretaking until they can grow into the beautiful people they are destined to be.

So, it's the night before the surgery.

I am in terror until I catch myself and realise my fear is having its way with me yet again, and I know I can be free of its pain. I force myself to breathe, so I take back my power over it, and I call my fear out and name it, demanding it leave me. I remind myself of the reality of fear. Fear is the ego part of my personality challenging me, making things look disastrous or dangerous to trigger me back into my natural state of innate faith. Sometimes that's where we get lost. Right now, I can't find my faith, so fear is challenging me big time.

I begin to breathe, breathing ever so deeply into the parts of my body that are feeling like fear. As I breathe deeply, I slow my breathing more and more to tell my body that I'm safe. I slow my breathing even further still and then I realise that the fear is abating. I can actually feel it disintegrating under the power that comes with each breath.

I remind myself that fear is my soul's way of getting my attention. It wants me to consciously choose my destiny path.

I know that when I don't choose, I choose by default.

There's not much point complaining about how things work out if I don't decide how I want *my* reaction to *my* world to be. I always say to my kids that there's the easy way to do things and the hard way. I know without a doubt I've been doing things the hard way by letting fear have control.

By breathing into the fear, I am simply deciding that something else is more important than the fear itself. If I let go, I can let the fear have its way with me, and I can once again choose to be in charge.

I understand that there is reason for every experience, and that although my intuition has guided me to have surgery over a fully natural healing, it does not make me a failure. I don't usually care what other people think, yet I realise in this moment that I'm worried about what people will think of me as a healer. I'm reminded of my ex-husband's 'jokes' that what I did was a load of rubbish, and that he hoped that my clients didn't wake up one day with the realisation that I was some sort of charlatan. Of course, his version was a little more colourful, but I'm sure you get the picture.

He was my greatest doubter; we saw the world very differently. And here I am with his words—decades later—still carrying great power over me. I am seeing myself as that very same charlatan, simply because I have cancer! If I'm not healing my cancer away, then what kind of a healer am I? I was a nurse and I am a healer. I know both modalities well and each has something to offer. I'm not anti-medicine, in fact, I'm not a fan of everything from either the medical or alternative health fields. I really believe that for any treatment to work, you have to have faith in it, and only then you will have the opportunity to heal. I don't believe in the necessity of all pharmaceutical and radiation treatments, but you can bet that if I've broken my arm, I'll be getting a doctor to set it.

The very best type of healer knows that a healer in a state of fear has no place conducting healing sessions for anyone! Upon my return from Hawaii, I struggled to be objective and my fears would pull me out of my state of centre (so essential for this line of work). I struggled at times to find the clarity and peace in the idea of healing such a large, rock hard tumour, and so I've chosen to get help. I can feel that this tumour is about to create metastases in my lungs. From a physical perspective, I need it out and I need it out now. I don't have time to sort out my fear or to take the time to physically break it down, as I would in the normal process of healing.

So, I have to choose right now. I have to choose a path of healing and it's okay for me to choose whatever I like. I have lived every day in an amplification of fear and terror as I grew up. Enough challenging and traumatic experiences have occurred in my life to give me justification for doing so, yet ...

Who do I want to be in charge of *my* destiny?

The only way I can be in charge is to choose my path along the way. And I can choose any path I like *and* change my mind if and when it suits me.

Fear vs. Faith

You can only have one at a time. We need to choose, it's as simple as that. You cannot have faith if you are feeling fear. They are not compatible. Fear will take you down the path of lack and limits and sadness and anger and end in self-criticism. We have to choose how we want our lives to be. Fear attracts *more* experiences that challenge you to find your faith. It feels terrible at times, and is even paralysing for some. It's hard to make any choice when you are in fear, but it *is* possible.

You cannot have fear if you are in a state of faith, for fear doesn't live there.

Fear and faith cannot co-exist in your mind.

You have to choose. What do you want to experience? Choose well.

When you don't choose one or the other, you are choosing fear by default. If you know fear, it can seem overwhelming to entertain the idea of living without it. Because by now, it is likely you have created quite the relationship with fear, it has become your companion, a friend of sorts.

A friend?

You've gotta be joking, I hear you say. Of course you don't see it like that! Who would actually want to live in the state of fear? No one, that's who! But have you looked at just how much you worry about things? At how much time you spend worrying? We actually *choose* to worry. How much time do you put into planning to avoid potential problems? No problems would be a great way to live, especially if it did not require the planning based on fears of what-if!

Now that you mention it, I can see fear is in my life a whole lot more than I'd like. Fear has become somewhat of a silent friend ...

To that I say, love yourself enough to put yourself first.

To love yourself well, fear *cannot* sit in the driver's seat. *You* need to be there. How many times have you not achieved your best, or missed an opportunity through fear? Fear of the what-ifs, fear of the maybes, fear of missing out or even the fear of achieving in itself. Fear of change has the greatest effect upon your destiny, as it's mostly undetectable. It's the one you barely notice as it has become familiar, almost like a friend.

To learn to love you, you must first understand your relationship with fear. When you understand how fear drives you, you put yourself firmly back into the driver's seat of your destiny. That is when you will be free of its chains, its limits and its will to keep you small and sad and struggling.

It is not necessary to defeat fear; it is far easier to embrace it, to encourage its presence, and to add it to your life rather than to further squash it. Fear makes life complicated and its demands upon your attention create a busy-ness that takes you away from your internal wisdom. You can literally feel it draining your focus away while dulling your greater intelligence. How many times have you berated yourself or become frustrated because you know 'stuff', or you know how to do, avoid or prevent the things that have happened?

You're shaking your head because it's so unlike you ... or is it? If it's happening more and more, perhaps fear is driving you more than you thought.

If you've given fear the driver's seat more often than you'd like, there's no point getting upset at yourself. You made a choice, but you can do it differently next time. Every day you get the opportunity to make hundreds or thousands of new choices. Start watching how you are making your choices and notice when fear arises.

If you make a choice from faith, you are choosing to feed yourself love. You'll find that if you keep choosing from faith, you'll start getting it right. Self-love is about creating the success, the ease and the joy that you see in others. It's about tapping into the secrets that will allow you to amplify your success. Choosing well is an essential ingredient in creating your success.

How do you know when fear is driving you and what can you do about it? How do you find the power and the strength and the confidence to walk away from the thundering voices of fear and into the abundance that comes with faith?

First, you need to understand fear. For the first four and a half years of my life, I knew no fear. I looked at life and could see a rhythm; everything had a place and everything balanced out. But as I grew, that began to change. I began to look to those around me for the example of how to experience life. I was curious and an avid learner, watching everything and everyone. I started to notice that people weren't living in the way I thought they should. It was so complicated. I noticed that they didn't see things or people or events that challenged them as a good thing.

I couldn't understand it. Wasn't it just this simple? That you are here to learn and not to suffer? I couldn't comprehend why they had to get so caught up in the drama of it all. Why could they not see how easy it was? When you learned the lesson, the situation went away. Why were they so focused upon the drama and the pain and the suffering that often came with it? Why couldn't they see that you never receive anything that you're not ready to learn?

When I was a child, it occurred to me that people were feeling this terrible emotion. I didn't really understand it. I tried to imagine that I could see it through their eyes, and then I found that I could, but I didn't like the feeling.

What they saw was disaster in some shape or form, and they were suffering as a result. They worried about outcomes and saw only the darkness of challenges. They couldn't see that light was always lying behind it, ready to bring joy into their lives.

I started to see so much of this, and once I started, I couldn't stop. It was like I became addicted to their fear and absorbed a truckload of their worries. As a result, I stopped seeing the way out of the darkness too.

Life became very worrying as I started to absorb the fear of others and live them too.

Once you've had a taste of fear, it's easy to let it take over. You forget how to let love fuel your choices.

When did it happen to you?

It's time to understand the source.

Self-love breeds confidence, and without confidence we struggle to conquer the fear that surrounds us. How does that happen? What are the reasons we stop loving ourselves? What gets in the way? There are a lot of reasons which contribute to poor or non-existent states of self-love, but they won't necessarily develop problems in everyone. For that to happen you will require these two triggers to occur close together.

1.   Mummy doesn't light up when she sees you, or when you enter a room.

It's incredible the difference a mother can make to a child. If she's present to the child rather than distracted by the dramas going on in her world, she will feel her heart fill with joy when she sees her child. That joy lights up her face and her eyes sparkle. The child feels their connection and the love that comes from it. It's that sparkle and love that feeds the child, automatically creating the network of mirroring that love in their own behaviour patterns.

But what if Mum is tired, and I mean really tired, or distracted? Perhaps she's not feeling well, or isn't coping, or perhaps she's been crying, or grieving, or is in conflict with her partner or someone close. Maybe she's anxious, or angry, or sad, or depressed or stressed. Perhaps she's looking at what her life has become and the reality has not matched up with her dreams. There's a myriad of reasons why Mum isn't lighting up for her child, and it may not be all the time.

That is only the first part in why you'll stop loving yourself. Here's the second and biggest trigger.

2.   Guilt!

If you are feeling sad, upset or empty because Mum isn't noticing you, and then someone reacts badly when you do something wrong, you have created the exact scenario to block your self-love. It's not your mother's fault (no one can be perfect all of the time), it's the way you react and the intensity of your guilt which creates the foundation for destroying your natural state of self-love. Each of us is born into that state of naturally loving who we are. If you experience something big or bad or there's a big reaction to your behaviour or crime, your guilt will corrupt the self-love pathways in the brain. The heart intelligence will respond by altering the capacity to self-love.

Guilt is one of the lowest vibrational emotional states, and it seeks to punish either you or those close to you, which then is a punishment to you too. Guilt becomes buried deep in your energy and is almost impossible to find.

The horror at causing a loved one anger or an upset as a result of your behaviour can be almost too much to bear. You become wracked with the pain of guilt, particularly if it was unintentional. The longer the guilt lasts without being processed, the more significant and greater the block on loving and nurturing yourself. If you have cuddles after saying sorry and are forgiven straight away, it'll drop right away. The problems arise because you're already feeling out of sorts at Mum for not 'loving' you, and now you feel ever so bad. At first there's the guilt, then the anger at yourself and soon enough there's something you can't remember that's making you feel bad inside. You only know it's to do with that person and you withdraw somewhat, creating the potential for further difficulties in your relationship.

So, not only do you now hurt inside, your hurt is now with that person and you don't understand why. You're not loving yourself because you feel bad inside, and you can't find what will make it better. If you disappointed your mother and the guilt stems from there, any woman (or girl) can stir the same feelings of guilt and inadequacy, further distancing yourself from the ability to love yourself. If it was your dad, any male can trigger you in the same way.

By now, you definitely won't remember why and it may even surprise you when you feel like you're overreacting to things that you've done wrong around that woman or man. This is because its cause has slipped into your subconscious.

I was sitting in a café with a young mum and her friend was across from me. The friend does not have a child and isn't that interested in the baby in the pram, yet the mum is managing to remain totally present to the friend's conversation while amusing her child. The child is occasionally disgruntled, yet as he's receiving her attention, he will not develop a self-love block. If, later in the evening, that same mum is tired, upset after arguing with her partner and has no energy or enthusiasm to give to another, the child will experience the first trigger to interrupt the pathways of self-love in the brain. If the child then spills his cup and dad is angry, you are now looking at both triggers being present, despite this child being less than a year old!

These triggers don't have to destroy your ability to love you, yet they place you in a hyper-attentive state. The problem with being in this state with these triggers in place, is that any number of events can concrete them into a self-love deficit, in other words, how worthy you feel of love.

If you cannot love yourself, you will not allow the love of others to feed you.

When you cannot love yourself, you will seek behaviours, people or environments that support your belief that you are unlovable, and so the cycle will continue.

Some of the most damaging triggers that cement a lack of self-worth, and thus the inability to self-nurture and love include:

- A trauma or traumatic event, particularly before the age of eight

- Disparagement from within the family

- Sibling rivalry and perceived favouritism of one child over another

- Negative comparisons favouring siblings or other children

- Bullying, from inside and/or outside the family

- Abuse: verbal, physical or sexual

- Fear of hurt or disaster

- Anxiety about loss

- Not being heard by those who matter

- Daddy doesn't notice your feelings

- Not allowed to speak

- Little or no success at the 'little things'

- Unrealistic demands of a child re: their achievements

- Made to be 'always wrong' and 'never right' by parents or parental figures

- People can't 'see' you

- Little or no recognition of that which makes you brilliant

- Made to do for others, at the expense of playing

- Needing to hide your intelligence/skills for safety or approval

- No space to be silent, imaginative and/or to grow

- No space to vision and create your ideas from an inability to see the world through joy

- Martyrdom

It's a pretty terrible sounding list, but I'm sure you can relate to at least a few things on it. What's great is that you can undoubtedly see some of these in your past, which means you're halfway there. You may not be able to remember the original triggers, as most triggers occur before the age of eight. It'd have to be pretty memorable or bad for you to remember.

The reality is that most of these triggers are things that 99.9% of parents would not see as 'big' things or mistakes they'd made in raising their children. Mostly, our triggers come from an internal sensitivity to our environment and how we're receiving the behaviour of those people who fill it. What we carry forward is unlikely to be our whole reality, but that does not negate the fact that at that time, it was a massive negative reality to the child we were.

The great news is that you don't need to remember everything in your past! I've taken this into account and the guided meditations in this book take care of the healing for you.

I've made it easy, certainly, but is it too easy?

I don't think that life needs to be hard, or that you should do things the hard way, so I've always focused upon creating 'ease' for my clients. Why should it be any different for you? I've purposely not published any of my previous books because it wasn't easy enough. This time it is.

I've created the exact technique for you to master your fear and put *you* back in charge. You can use it each day. The next guided meditation will realign your nervous system to healthy function, enabling you to manage your fear in everyday situations, along with reorientating your self-love pathways. Both techniques will need to be used frequently, at least initially, until you can comfortably walk through life with ease.

So, let's go!

How to Master Fear

1. Identify

2. Release

3. Choose

4. Breathe!

It really is that simple and it will only take you a few minutes. Soon you'll be the master of your fear and back in the driver's seat of your destiny!

Become very aware of how you're feeling, notice it in all of your experiences. When you find you're in fear, take a big deep breath and put fear on notice.

Say: "I can see you fear! You are my old pattern of behaviour. I'm choosing to do it differently, starting right now!"

Feel and allow your power to grow as it releases from the fear. Choose: Do you want to live in the fear or do you want freedom from it?

Say: "I choose to live without limits right now, to release my fear and to embrace my inner faith with every breath."

Find where you're feeling the fear in your body. Imagine that you can breathe there. Breathe into the place you're feeling it, until it dissolves away. Feel for any other places in the body which are holding your fear and breathe into them in the same way.

As you do, know that each breath carries joy, and with it, the power of this choice into each of those same spots in the body that previously felt the fear, changing their vibration and thus your experience.

This empowers you to be more of yourself, more of who you want to be and puts you back in charge of your destiny.

Meditation: Retuning the Nervous System for Rapid Change

Do this meditation every day for a month, then at least once a week.

Read or speak it slowly, with pauses at the end of sentences. Take yourself to a quiet space where you'll not be interrupted for a while. Turn off your phone, close the door and get yourself comfortable.

It's time to breathe, to let go.

We're going to help your nervous system to cope with the rapid changes of your world and your life.

As you breathe, you are slowing each breath.

In through the nose ... out through the mouth.

There's no need to be afraid anymore.

Each and every breath is making you more and more relaxed.

As you breathe, you feel your breath almost passing through the confines of your lungs.

It's almost as if you can breathe anywhere in the body.

Breathing slower and slower ... your body knows now that it is safe.

Each and every breath makes you feel even safer.

As you breathe, you find your breath is naturally going into the heart.

Your heart responds with such joy and peace with each and every breath.

You can feel your internal intelligence and wisdom being awakened as your body is dropping into peace.

Your body is beginning to really relax and is becoming heavier in your chair or where you're lying.

You notice any parts of your body that are feeling fear and you imagine you can breathe into them.

Every breath is dissipating the fear ... you can feel peace flowing through your body.

Your body is relaxed.

Your mind is relaxed.

You are at ease now with the process, you know only good will come to you now.

You become aware of your brain, resting gently within your skull and you can feel so much activity.

As you breathe deeper and deeper, you feel waves of love coming from your heart into your brain.

Your brain is beginning to calm, and the busy-ness is slowing down.

Ever so slowly the brain is slowing down.

You intrinsically know that your intelligence is lifting with each and every breath.

As each time you breathe, you are disintegrating the power that fear has over you.

You breathe deeply into your heart and its waves of love expand even bigger than before.

This love is so very strong.

As the love moves through the brain, it is disintegrating the darkness away from your internal light.

You know that this light is that which carries your inner wisdom, your innate intelligence.

And you now feel it moving downwards through your spinal cord.

You can feel where your spinal cord reaches from the base of the brain down through your spine in the centre of your back, down to your bottom.

The light is filling every part of it.

You can feel this brilliant light, the carrier of your inner wisdom.

Your innate intelligence is moving now from the spine outwards.

Through the spinal nerves into the body.

The spinal nerves reach from every part of your spinal cord and create little branches of nerves that divide and extend into every part of your body.

You can feel this brilliant light, the carrier of your inner wisdom.

Your innate intelligence moving now through each of the nerve branches.

Until you are filled with light.

It feels like nothing you've ever experienced before.

This light feels like it is an integral part of your nerves.

And the systems of the body it reaches.

As you breathe even deeper, you watch the light begin to change its colour into a brilliant emerald green.

And you see it beginning to heal old misunderstandings.

The triggers and the guilt and the sadness and the anger are unable to withstand the brilliance of the light.

And they disappear as you watch.

As you watch the light, you see the green is deepening around your heart.

And you feel such love as it melts away old wounds.

You breathe deeper and deeper and you know that in this moment you are eternally safe.

That no matter what the world brings you, you will be safe inside.

And nothing can hurt in the way it did before.

You find that you are fascinated with what is happening with the deepening of the emerald green energy at the heart.

As you watch, you see the golden glow of joy beginning to vibrate outward, from the heart.

And there are now streams of gold throughout your body.

You feel the joy bubbling through you, and it may even bring tears to your eyes at the brilliance of it.

Still, you are fascinated with what is happening in the heart, as the joy builds through the body.

You can see something incredible is happening.

As you watch the heart becomes enormous and looks silvery like a mirror.

As you watch the reflection of the heart, you can see great waves of self-love returning into the core of the heart.

With every breath, the heart is becoming more solid, with faith and a certainty of your innate safety no matter what you will face.

You can feel such a peace creating waves through all of your energy until you are tingling all over.

Each breath makes you tingle even more.

Your heart is now the only thing you can see.

For it has become a brilliant rose-coloured pink.

So filled with your own love.

The love you create to sustain your dreams.

To sustain your creativity and passion.

To sustain your ability to make magic in your world.

Dreams feel possible, goals a reality.

You know now that you have reconnected to your internal wisdom, your innate intelligence.

You know that you are fed by the richness of your self-love.

That you can do or be anything now.

You can't feel the pressure of before.

You know you are enough and that you can handle anything that comes.

You finally believe in you.

The room and its sounds creep back into your awareness and you find you are once again in the room.

Breathing deeply, you open your eyes and take a moment to integrate how you feel. You drink some water.

You imagine your feet connecting with the energy of the earth below you, anchoring you back into your body.

You can rise slowly and return to your day or settle into sleep, knowing you are always going to be okay.

Surgery

My eyes fly open on the morning of the surgery well before my alarm, despite it being set so ridiculously early. I'm glad of it. The sun is just beginning to rise and the only sound in the street is the singing of the birds. I soak it in; this may be the last time I get to hear it. I focus on feeling the energy of each of our three kids who are still living here with us and then the two who live in their own places. One by one, I embrace them and send them my love, hoping they can feel it, and wishing I had more time and given them all more cuddles. What if I never get to hug them again? I look over at Berni and am ever so grateful for his love and support last night.

Inside of me, my deep internal wisdom tells me that this is the wandering of the ego, and that I will once again be at home, able to cuddle and love my children and this beautiful man many times over. I breathe into the moments of fear as they arise, using the mastery of fear techniques I've been teaching for years, and it abates and disappears. I remember Berni's arms around me and it was as if I could literally feel the love pumping through them and into me, as I explained my fears to him.

I told him of the seriousness of the surgery and that I may not survive the procedure. I told him of the myriad of side effects that can occur (without going in to too much detail so that I didn't terrify him completely), that could mar or delay my recovery. I told him I was hoping that all would be well and I would do my best to go into the surgery as calm and relaxed as I could. I had several healers who were planning to spend various parts of the day sending me distant healing to keep me stable, with others sending healing to Berni and the children. Lachy was getting himself and Zavier off to school, Maddie was with her boyfriend and Dylan and Elyse were planning to stay with Berni at the hospital for the duration of the surgery.

As I lay there listening and thinking of the impending surgery, Berni rolls over on cue to wrap me once again into his arms. The tears begin to flow.

"What if ..."

"It's not going to happen love, we both know you're going to make it."

I smile at his ever-knowing of me, although I can see his tears matching mine. He is just lying beside me, staring at me, bathing me with his love when the alarm finally goes off. It feels like time has stood still and we've been here forever.

I'm already packed, so after a quick shower, wistful looks and kisses at the boys and a cuddle for my little dog, Jack, I walk out the door. I am in tears as we drive away, not knowing exactly what my future holds, but with a pretty good idea of what will happen. The ability to see the future can sometimes be a curse.

I proceed through the admission clinic, finding it difficult to believe this could be my last day of life, despite my fears. Berni is with me all the way as they take blood, wrap me in a warmer blanket that pumps air around my body, and connect me to their machines. They give us privacy by wrapping the curtains around us and I'm grateful.

I'm also scared, but as I apply my fear master techniques, it abates with each breath. My body automatically knows what to do now. We kiss goodbye. I tell Berni I love him so much, that I'm so grateful for all of his support and for the great love we've had together. He can barely speak and tells me he loves me so much.

They wheel me away from him.

I don't know how I'll be when I see him next, and I try not to think of the last patient I nursed with this condition who died on the operating table. The immediacy of the flurry of people and the activity that surrounds me takes my attention away.

I am now focusing upon my breath, as Debra, my very reassuring anaesthetist, explains everything they're doing as they go. She rang me yesterday and went step by step through each of the processes I can expect, reassured me that David was the best, that I would be fine, that he was a great surgeon and that she fully expects to see me fit and well on the other side of the surgery. She reassures me that it's her job to keep me alive and well during the surgery, so I can relax in her hands. It's the first time someone other than Berni has made me feel this safe in decades.

As the needles go in and machines are attached, I focus upon the meditative state I usually slip into so easily. As the anaesthetist puts me to sleep, and it is met by the meditative state rising up to greet it. I release my body and my life into their very good hands.

"Karina, Karina, Karina ..."

There is this insistent voice pulling me back into my body from the blissful place of light that I've been.

I'm in the recovery room, attached to more tubes than I can count. I have an oxygen mask over my face and I feel like I've just emerged from the longest of meditations. I'm alert and awake and not groggy at all.

I feel healed.

The nurse tells me that all has gone well and I'm doing great. The anaesthetist emerges and her smile tells me as much as her words. "You did great, they got it all and you were the most stable patient I've ever had. None of your vitals moved at all, you barely lost any blood and you didn't need a transfusion." She has ordered medications to manage my pain and nausea and I'll be heading to the intensive care ward for a few days until I'm stable. I thank her and she moves on with her day, knowing she'll check on me as we go.

David emerges and looks like he's just been given the best present ever. "We got it all, it doesn't look like anything else was affected, but to be safe I've taken anything that was adhered to the tumour. You've lost most of your left adrenal gland and about 25 cm of intestine, but I was able to join the ends successfully. You did not need a colostomy."

He looks so happy, but is also shaking his head at just how stable my body had been in surgery. I tell him that was the healers I had sending me healing. I'm not sure if he is perplexed at that possibility, or just how awake and alert I am. I ask him how long it has taken as he walks away, and he says it was only 4.5 hours.

It was pretty much perfect!

I know Berni knows now that I'm out, as David has already spoken to him. I can feel his love and relief and his impatience to see me, but he will have to wait. It takes time for me to be transferred into intensive care (ICU), and they take about an hour to do their stuff while connecting me and my million tubes to their machines. Berni is on his own when he comes in, which is unsurprising. He wouldn't want to share this moment, and both Elyse and Dylan returned to work once the news came through. I am to be on strictly limited visitors for the time being.

His face is full of joy and tears and relief, and love and a flash of fear crosses his face as he sees the reality of me among the oxygen mask and tubing and machines. They seem to be everywhere. I am dwarfed by enormous heat blankets being pumped full of warm air to bring my body temperature back up to normal. I look tiny.

I'm feeling groggy now as the medications for pain and nausea are taking effect.

I feel such love for this man and relief. He's coping with the medical stuff and the hospital well, it seems. Just seeing him makes me deeply relaxed and I fall into a deep sleep. Each time I wake he's there, and he's the only person I want to see. The ICU is very busy and very noisy, and he reluctantly leaves that evening to care for the children. I sleep on and off.

The next day he's back by my side and after school, Lachy and Zavier are there too. I have shown them a myriad of stock advertising images of patients in the ICU so they would know what to expect. Despite the potential for it to be frightening for them, I feel they'll cope better if they can see I'm doing okay. Lachy's face lights up with such joy when he sees me, and I get tentative hugs from both of the boys. We've taken the oxygen mask off for a little while my levels are good, so as to look more normal for them. They've not had a nine-year-old in the ICU, so everyone is being super great and reassuring with their smiles and words.

Lachy would tell me later that he'd been prepared for seeing me with my descriptions and photos, but he hadn't been prepared for the reality of seeing other intubated and extremely ill patients who looked as if they were about to die. When he saw me, it was with such relief to see me conscious, as he then knew I would make it.

Zavier turns to his iPad and makes me an 'I love you' image. I ask him if he's okay and he tells me that I was wrong, I am not grey at all.

Thank you, Hawaii, what a wonderful tan!

Dylan and Maddie hate hospitals with a vengeance since Nanna died in one, but they brave it. Dylan tells me I'm looking better than he thought. Berni just can't take his eyes off me. Every time I wake, he's right there, loving me with his big smile, and his presence soothes me.

The ICU passes in a blur of noise and machines beeping and needles and I'm almost ready to go back to the ward. They've had trouble with my epidural and the stability of the numbness of the anaesthetic block.

I started on food right away and it didn't take me long to figure out something wasn't right with my stomach. I told David on his visit and he tells me I have a bile leak into my abdomen and will be unable to eat anything with fat in it for three weeks. I'm remaining as positive with everything as I can. I am alive, and if that's the worst I have to do, then so be it.

I'm suffering from nausea, still saying my stomach isn't working and they're giving me medications for it. I have all the signs that tell them that my intestine has returned to full function, so they assume it is to do with the medications or the bile leak. Three days after my admission to the ICU, the epidural and arterial lines are removed and I am readied for transfer to the high dependency surgical ward. I press the button to give myself a dose of the pain infusion.

Before I reach the ward, I am hit in the elevator with the most incredible pain that literally takes my breath away. I think I'm going to faint. I am beyond dizzy with the intensity of it. I'm already lying down, so I press the button again, but the medication is not taking away the pain. Berni is with me as always and starts to give me healing as I'm rushed to the ward. There is a flurry of activity to get me comfortable and pain and nausea free. My abdomen is so bloated that I look bigger than before the surgery.

Surely this can't be right? I remain under observation until it becomes clear.

I'm allowed to have visitors now although we are still keeping it very limited. The healers who have been caring for me, the kids and close family are given permission for short visits. Alesa comes in with crystals and is so relieved to see me. Peta comes in and does the old-fashioned nursing techniques for comfort that we'd learnt together, and tut-tuts about the state of things. John comes in with his smile and love and sits beside Berni, happy to see me.

I've been feeling so nauseous and I respond to his smile by projectile vomiting the largest amount of green semi-solid fluid you've ever seen all over myself, the bed, and then finally, another

1500 ml into a vomit bag. The nurse is in shock at just how much fluid was there; as are we, as I'd only vomited three times! It looks like there's more than a litre of vomit all over the bed. Suddenly, my pain is gone.

As Berni and John head downstairs to have a cuppa, I drag myself to the shower again so the nurse and I can try to clear it out of my hair. Oh, I wish I'd had a haircut before I came! I am surprised that John returns, cracking a joke as always. Honestly, that vomit was enough to end the friendship of millions!

I am moved into a single room in response to my massive vomit, and am feeling pretty drugged by the strong anti-nausea medication I now have in my IV. My sister, Bec, brings my mother down from the country to visit, which is quite a miracle. She hates Melbourne and her health doesn't allow her to travel on long trips. I put on a brave face as she fluffs around my room, grateful she's made it down. We'd allowed a couple of close friends to visit, and as they arrive, you can see how I'm doing on their faces. I know I'm not looking well, yet by the time they leave they're telling me how amazed they are that I'm doing this well this quickly.

I smile at them, but on the inside, I'm feeling near the worst I've felt.

Alas, visitors apart from the children are once again off limits, as I deteriorate further. Berni is sending out updates as things change via text to the many friends and family who are worried. Rightfully so at the moment.

The vomiting has started again, 1500 ml each time, and I can't move without feeling like I'll vomit again. I have to try so hard to look only tired for Zavier when he visits. I'm trying not to traumatise him, but then I'm so sick I can't think of anyone or anything. Berni is with me all day, and there's a roster of care and meals being provided by my school friends for the family.

When Berni leaves each night, I am in tears. I need him to stay, I need him to make it better as I feel so very sick. He drags himself away and I am left with the nurses. Their care is good, yet I am ever so sick and nothing is making me better. I can feel the healing being sent to me, but the sickness is intensifying. David is in each day, as is the physician, and they're both shaking their heads as to what's going on. He's referring to his colleagues in other states and countries for ideas as to the source, but no one has seen this. I am an anomaly.

The anaesthetic pain specialist Jason is my only light in the day, as he visits each morning before Berni arrives. He's so lovely and we have a lot in common. We seem to spend a heap of time talking each day, as he is managing my pain and nausea medications. He's the kind of guy that if circumstances were different, could have been a friend. He smiles and chats and distracts me from the immediacy of my situation, and I love him for it. Yet I am still so sick.

Soon there is nothing else to be done other than to take me back to theatre. The CT scans show that while the bowel is working lower down where the surgery was, there appears to be something wrong with my stomach!

I return from surgery with a chipped area on the inside of my front tooth, a seriously raw throat and two tubes into my nose. One is to drain my stomach, the other is set deep into the intestine to feed me. I have lost so much weight and I've nothing in me to feed me the nutrients I need to heal. The dietician is beside herself trying to manage my care. The procedure was technically difficult, and it took multiple approaches to detect the issues and get the tubes in place. I spend a terrible night unable to sleep and having severe hallucinations, no doubt due to the anaesthetic drugs in my system.

I'm so glad to have a diagnosis, but alas, now begins what could be a very long journey. Due to the difficulty of access to the tumour during the initial surgery, my stomach had been heavily handled and has become paralysed as a result. It could take months to recover its nervous function and heal.

I sink into a deep depression as things only get worse.

The feeds begin and don't agree with me; constant diarrhoea and an instance of incontinence have me humiliated and beaten. Berni is with me all the time and I'm having to use the toilet in front of him. He doesn't seem to care. He tells me he loves me. "You're alive and we'll do whatever it takes to get you better, don't worry love."

The days tick over into weeks and still I'm not getting better.

Lachy has the formal dance with a date from his former school and I miss it. He sends me photos and I'm in tears. Maddie has told me she's found her ideal flat after months of looking and will soon be moving out. I was supposed to be home a week ago. Zavier has his school concert in a week and I'm so upset at the thought of missing it.

I'm finding it so hard and Berni is struggling to manage supporting the kids at home while running the house, so he has the odd evening at home. Lachy has been doing heaps, including school pick-ups and after school activities despite his heavy schedule of exams and deadlines. Maddie is helping on the days she isn't working and Dylan is calling at least twice a day to make sure Berni's doing okay, and to help sort out what needs to be done.

My original planning had been for ten days. It is now weeks.

Tonight, Berni is at home and Maddie is sitting with me, encouraging me and holding my hand. I'm not sure she realised just how sick I was, but she sure knows now. I'm lying ever so still, trying not to vomit as I ask her about her new flat. I listen as she details every single thing she's done or has to do. Her voice is comforting and I relax for a while till I'm ready for sleep.

When David comes in to visit in the morning, I'm crying. It's the first time I've failed to be positive about my situation. I've had so little sleep at night since my surgery, what with the constant attention from the nurses. He listens through my tears and then everything changes. I am not to be disturbed during the night unless I call to the nurses. I will go to Zavier's concert if I want to, he can make that happen. Soon, everything is focused upon getting the feeds and me right to get me to the concert. My friend Kat is the principal of the junior school, and makes it happen from her end.

The day arrives. As we drive away from the hospital, I am struck with fear and need to go back. I have become hospitalised and don't feel safe without its care, its routines and sounds. Bern pulls over, takes my hands and looks at me. "I can take you back anytime you like darling and I will, but you can do this. I need you to try for me."

I breathe into my fear using the mastery techniques and it eases, and before I know it, we arrive at the school. I haven't seen Zavier for three days as he's been sick too, and he's just as excited as I am.

As I arrive, Kat comes to the car and gives me a hug. She's happy to see me and she's teary, and so am I. She has an exact timing of the entire schedule so that I can attend for just Zavier's items. I'm wheeled into the foyer and find she's rearranged her VIP seating so that Berni can sit in her row next to me and I will be closer to the stage in the aisle. I am in a wheelchair with freshly washed hair, mascara, contacts and a pale lippy, but I have two tubes coming out of my nose. They have spigots in them to block them off and are tucked under my blanket, yet there's no mistaking that I am a very sick woman.

As I'm settled in the auditorium, the sounds of bagpipes and then drums begin to stream around me. The college is such a special and supportive school and I've been so grateful for the extra care of Lachy and Zavier during my illness. The children who are waiting near me are so respectful, smiling at me in encouragement.

The school teaches the military tattoo and it's so very touching to hear it at every special occasion. They march in playing and assemble on stage, and Kat uses the distraction to wheel me in.

I am crying in gratitude that I'm there.

Kat is blocking my wheelchair from rolling with her heels, as one of the brakes is not working. I nod to show that I'm okay as both she and Berni squeeze my hands. Their next song is Hallelujah, made famous by the wonderful Leonard Cohen, and I can't stop crying, I'm just so overcome with happiness to be there.

And then in a flash of colour, Zavier and his friends have filled the stage. Kat has me as close as I can be, and she's pointing to him that I'm there. His face lights up in joy and he puts on the best performance of his life. At that moment, any embarrassment of people seeing me so pale and unwell with tubes out my nose, disappears instantly. I would have done anything for this moment for my child.

After his four songs, Kat pulls me back into an alcove as his class pours down the aisle to exit. The kids are excited to see me and wave as they pass, and then she suddenly grabs Zavier out of the line. He looks startled until he sees she's hiding me, ready for cuddles. He hugs me hard and tells me he loves me and it's just one of those magic moments. I'm able to tell him how brilliant he is, and as he walks away, everything changes.

My drive to recover and return home is reawakened.

When I return to hospital, someone is having a heart attack and the ward is under a code blue. Without the nurses, Berni and I spend some sacred time together and I feel myself coming back into my body in response to his love. I have felt so disconnected and outside of my body since the surgery. I'd tried hard to heal myself, but my healing ability disappeared the day I went to surgery.

Following the concert, I have visits and healing from Alesa, Peta, John and Di. Each would heal a different aspect as to why I wasn't healing, and why my stomach was still paralysed, which together with Berni's daily healing and love, would assist me to recover.

Three days after the concert, I appear to have had a miraculous healing. All of a sudden, I could see myself out of the hospital. I was having daily dates with Berni out of the ward in the hospital cafe, and it was making a huge difference. My tubes were decreasing their output and I was managing food without nausea or vomiting. On the last morning, David is blown away that I have managed to eat a whole meal without nausea and says I can go home after lunch if all is still well. I can't wait and phone Berni to tell him. I wake him as doctors do their rounds super early, but I don't think he's ever been so happy to be awake.

Today he gets to take his great love home!

After twenty-two days in hospital, the tube is out and I'm on the way. We realise we better tell the people who are planning to visit that day. John is delighted and happy to make new plans for his afternoon. Berni takes me to what has become our post hospital/tests/appointments café in Richmond. I have my first real chai and eat a small lunch.

Still no nausea!

I ring Dylan to let him know and thank him for looking after his dad so well for me. He's stoked! I send a text to Lachy to say hello and to find out if he'd be home for a delivery I was expecting and he says he'll be home in an hour, that he's on the way to the gym for a quick session.

Little Jack, our black King Charles Cavalier spaniel, greets me at the door and doesn't want to let me go. I'm in tears as I sit down to cuddle him, he's so attached to me in this moment.

It's so nice to be home! Maddie phones to see if I need anything and I suddenly remember she's on her way to the hospital after picking up her apartment keys. She's just got her apartment! I say it depends on when and where she's coming. When she hears that I'm home her squeal is deafening and can be heard everywhere. Jack's barking and she's on her way!

I lay on the bed to rest while we wait for Lachy. It's already been such a big day and I am still weak and tired throughout the day. I hear him come in, chatting on the phone, and I walk in my socks to the landing. He hangs up from his call as he starts up the stairs. "Don't you hug your mum anymore when you walk in the door?" I say when he's almost at the top.

He looks up, goes white, and then swears and continues to swear, even as he's gingerly hugging me. He is obviously happy to see me, as he wasn't expecting me home for a few days. Seeing me talking to him at the top of the stairs put him in a fright. He assumed I must have died and that this was my ghost talking to him.

We blame it on Berni, because he couldn't be angry with me as he was so happy to have me home.

Berni picks up Zavier early from his play-over and he's a bit grumpy, so Bern bribes him with a Slurpee on the way home. As he walks into the door, Zavier immediately sees me. "I'm home!" I squeal and he comes running. It's like he's never going to let me go. Soon almost everyone is there but Elyse, who's in New York on yet another trip.

Bern and I can't stop smiling at each other. As I settle into our bed, I feel so happy, so safe and so glad that I have made it.

There was little joy in this hospital journey. It has challenged me beyond what I thought myself capable of and been harder than anything I've ever had to do. As I settle to sleep, I realise it's the first night I've had in my bed without cancer for a very long time.

Life Comes in Pairs

Do you ever wonder how you got to this moment? Where life might have taken you if you'd made one different choice? If you'd made *any* choice differently? Would you be happy? If I'd not chosen my ex-husband, I would never have given birth to our two children. I can't imagine living without Maddie and Lachy, and while it might be quieter, my life would be definitely lacking. But were they really worth the difficulties of that marriage and what became of me in it? Would I choose it again?

Absolutely! I love those kids and I would hate to live one day without them.

Life coming in pairs is demonstrated quite aptly in the movie *Sliding Doors*. It stars Gwyneth Paltrow, who as a result of being fired from her job, rushes to catch the early train home. Scenes from two parallel lives show the outcomes of either making the train or missing it. It's fascinating to watch. In the first life, she makes the train, chats to a guy on the train (who she had met earlier in the day in an elevator), and then arrives home to find her lover in bed with another woman. She leaves the lover and tries to put her life back together, starting something of a romance with the man on the train.

In the second life, she misses the train. She is hurt by a mugger while trying to catch a cab, and so arrives home after the woman has left. In the second life, her lover continues to juggle both women as she juggles two jobs to make ends meet.

In both lives she finds out she is pregnant, and a myriad of circumstances see her admitted to hospital after an accident. In each life, she loses her baby. At the end of the hospitalisation in the second life, she drops an earring in an elevator and has a connecting conversation with the man from the train. It appears that they will come together romantically in this life, as they had in the first.

In each version of her life many of the same things happened, such as ending up pregnant, losing her baby and having the opportunity to be with the man on the train. In the end, she didn't miss out on the outcomes despite her choices or the path she followed.

If I'm right and our lives are like that movie, we will all end up at the same point eventually. Almost a dozen times my life has almost crossed paths with Berni's life and yet we never knowingly met. Perhaps we wouldn't have had success in this great love of ours if we'd become involved earlier. Perhaps we both needed our first marriages to help us learn what we really wanted and needed in a relationship, which would then enable us to see the brilliance in each other.

So, we each have a destiny, and you'll find a myriad of pathways that will get you there. Think of the ancient medieval saying, "All roads lead to Rome." If we're going to end up at same spot (dying), shouldn't we make the most of each and every day we have here? There's nothing like surviving cancer or a trauma or an abusive relationship to give you the drive to make the most of each day.

How many of us really know how to create joy and brilliance and opportunity each day? Many of us just feel lucky enough to have survived the day. Not everyone is loving how their days are, or love living their life. Many are disappointed. Maybe you're missing someone you love or someone to love. Maybe your job isn't stimulating or you don't have a job. The list is endless.

The best way to affect your destiny is to make conscious choices. How we choose can make an enormous difference to the outcomes.

In every moment of every day, we have two choices: *respond* or *react!*

How many times have you berated yourself for reacting in a

way that was over the top, inappropriate, or just not reflective of who you are as a person? How many times have you wished in retrospect that you said nothing, said more, said something or said it differently? When we react, it seems like what happens occurs almost spontaneously without our input, yet this is not true. Our reaction stems from the fears we've absorbed over lifetimes. When we respond, it sources from a place of wisdom somewhere inside.

The wisdom choices obviously sound like a better choice, but how can we choose from wisdom when we don't understand where it comes from, or where to access it? Is this wisdom the result of the learnings of our lifetimes, or is it bigger than that? Think of a time when you took a breath, and could actually make a choice that reflected who you were inside.

It wasn't made from a place of fear, was it?

It came from the calmness within, almost like a gut instinct or a feeling. You were actually using your intuition to access that wisdom and to drive your destiny. As a child, you learn pretty quickly how to react to get your own way. It takes no time at all to work out whether or not a tantrum will work. You either get attention, discipline, or you get your own way. It teaches you by example that to get your own way what you need to do is *react*. This creates your pattern for the future.

In the same way, you can learn how to *respond* using your wisdom, such as when you're climbing a tree, for instance. Each time you place your foot on a branch, your intuition accesses your wisdom to decide just how far to go. Each time you feel yourself teeter, or the branch begin to give out underneath you, your intuition connects to where you are and keeps you safe. Learning to harness those same instinctive skills with your intuition will lead you down the road to success. It will be faster and easier than you ever imagined possible.

Every time we try something new it feels awkward and difficult, but if you do it enough times it becomes routine, and before you know it, you don't need to even think about the process. When was the last time you thought about tying shoelaces or riding a bike or making cereal or cooking toast? There are so many things we do automatically without the need for active thinking to make it happen. Each time you master an activity, you create a muscle memory in your brain. Without even thinking about it, you've built up a library of wisdom that supports you as you need it.

In the last meditation chapter, we used the guided meditation to retune your brain and the reactions of your body to fear. Now that your brain is not spending all its energy on managing your fear, it is reprogramming itself to match your new way of being.

Every new choice is making new pathways of behaving to match your new reality.

What this means is that the next time you face a situation that previously would have caused you fear, your brain and body will now pull upon your new muscle memories. These memories source out of your new wisdom choices through your intuition and become your first path of response. While you sleep, old unused pathways are being cleared to make room for the new.

Mastering fear is so incredible and its reach is further than you might imagine. Choosing to *respond* rather than *react* once you've mastered fear becomes the easiest thing in the world. Yes, initially it feels clunky and awkward and not too comfortable. It's just like learning a language or riding a bike; it's strange to begin with but once you've got it, you've got it. Fluency is easy to master because you're not worrying about failing or how hard it is, you're just doing it. Practicing and mastering your fear is so important. It's great, because at the beginning, it'll feel like you've got a bagful of opportunities.

So, how do we do it?

It is actually easier than you think. It's amazing just how calm you can be when fear is no longer your master.

For instance, I've just had another check-up with my surgical oncologist for the results of my latest CT scan. I'm having them more regularly than I'd like, as I struggle to manage the radiation from the scan, and find it takes me a week to recover. Despite the results being available immediately, Berni and I receive them at my appointment a couple of days later. This situation is a really good example of how you can do things the easy way or the hard way. The results will be the same, regardless of whether I stress and worry, or wait patiently.

The easy way is to breathe into any fear that comes up, knowing it is challenging me to reach into deeper levels of faith. I know that if I step into that quiet place inside me and I breathe deeply, I can access my internal wisdom. If I do so, I can connect through my intuition and know that the test results will be as we expect, negative. If the worst was to happen and they were positive, I know I'm perfectly equipped to deal with whatever may come. I never face anything I can't handle. I can sleep and I can enjoy the days that lead up to the appointment.

The hard way is to let fear have the reins and tell me all the disastrous possibilities—that I have cancer again and that I will no doubt die. If I let fear be in charge, I will be grumpy or snappy, focusing on the negative and attracting more negativity towards me. Nothing will be right and I'll be stressing and worrying and planning for the worst to come. In no time at all, I'll be imagining my own funeral, my digestion will have seized up, I'll feel sick and be unable to sleep. The results will be the same and in the meantime, I would've made a mess of at least today and quite possibly a few days or weeks before. What is true is that I have created my own suffering.

What's also true is that we're all human and fear is our constant companion. I'm not suggesting for a moment that you have to live this perfect life without fear. What I'm suggesting is that life is a whole lot better if you learn to *manage* it. You do not have to become some sort of saint, just watchful. When you are watchful, you are in charge of your choices. We can't always change the situations we'll face in life, but we can change how we experience them. It's all a matter of perspective. Know that there are always two ways of managing things; the easy way, and the way I did it for decades of my life—the hard way!

Finally, there's *perspective* to look at. It's so funny how ten people can have ten different versions of the same incident, and yet all ten versions are right. It is their truth, how they saw what happened. When I was first diagnosed with cancer, most people saw my death or great suffering. They were picturing me having some version of chemotherapy; losing my hair, suffering radiation burns and very, very thin.

In fact, I had people telling me (or I'd hear them talking behind my back) about how I should have chemotherapy and that I was making a big mistake by not having it. Some people were incredibly opinionated, but it was coming from their limited past experience, rather than any real knowledge of my diagnosis.

My type of cancer is so rare that doctors haven't got a handle on it, yet some people assumed they knew better. My cancer doesn't respond to chemotherapy, and so therefore, it wasn't an option. I think that's enough said.

Each of those people is reacting to the news of my cancer from a space of what they currently know. A lack of information combined with old or inaccurate knowledge can only contribute to the fear or the difficulty of those walking the path through cancer.

Anyone who has a cancer diagnosis will tell you it's a very difficult journey, and that surviving it is only one half of the struggle. The diagnosis and the reactions of others and the constant need for follow-up means that you're living with it every day. Every little pain or issue you feel in your body has you imagining the cancer is back and you're on your deathbed in minutes.

That is a *reaction* and that is your choice.

Today, I'm choosing to *respond*, knowing that I can't do anything about the news right now. I know that if I'm looking after myself and I'm in a good space, then I'll be in a good position to deal with whatever I'm told. I won't be too tired to celebrate, and I'll be in a better frame of mind if the news is challenging.

Responding just seems like the better way. When reaction was my choice, I wasn't great to be around. Things were always a drama and I was always reliving and discussing the current drama with my friends, building it up even bigger than it was. Drama is fed by fear, and reacting is a great way of fast-tracking both.

If I'm choosing to respond, I know that there is a lesson in each and every challenge, and that this one is no different. Panic is of no benefit to anyone.

If I can remain calm and focus on the lesson, I can have an entirely different experience. We have been constantly praised by people who are incredulous that we can remain so positive and calm about my circumstances. But that's exactly it, they're *my* circumstances until I work out what I need to learn, and only then can the circumstance change, leave or disappear. Do I need a new skill? Or is it wisdom that I need to develop? Manage that and you've got it made. Life is just easier.

In every single thing that I face, I use this method. I first deal with any fear, then I become still and quiet in my mind and I ask myself, "What is the lesson? What do I need to learn or develop?" In the stillness, I'll find my answers. In the quiet I'll get an idea of what needs to be the next step. Then I'll take a big, deep breath, I'll face my fears and I'll do it anyway.

Living a life of fear, with its lack and limits, is not the way I want to live. When I die, you can be sure I won't be lying there with regrets. I'll have lived life to the full. I might be worn out, and maybe even a bit broken, but it will have been a life well lived!

So, what are you going to do now? Choose to respond as you face each challenge? Or react to your fear? I like that this is the one thing that we're in charge of and can control. When you get used to it, it becomes fun choosing. Best of all, you can choose any way you like.

The only thing that's certain in life is that you have a choice in how you experience things. No one can take that away from you.

P.S. The results of my scan were (of course!) cancer free. I can almost hear my intuition saying, "I told you so!"

Action!
Sourcing the Hatred

The ability to even discern that you are living in any degree of self-hatred is a tricky thing. Self-hatred comes with a secret—it's not a secret to everyone, but it is a secret to the wearer—they cannot see it within themselves. They imagine themselves to be happy, yet they do not know just how much happiness they could experience. In the quiet times (assuming they find the quiet), they can find that they are unhappy and that there is a yearning for more.

"I'm lonely as hell, despite being the envy of those around me. I have success in everything, but I envy the human connection I can see in others, the success of their love."
— L.D., Melbourne

What they cannot easily define is the source of their misery, for on the surface they have nothing 'real' to complain about. Many are the envy of their friends as they appear to have it all, yet true happiness seems evasive. It is something seen on the faces of others, in books and in the movies ... something you would only ever dream of for yourself.

Others can see the good in you. You have ever so much potential that you can't see! I've been healing people for a long time on their internal states of self-love vs. self-hatred, and what I have found in *everyone* is one common theme.

You have made an enemy of yourself.

You are being cruel to yourself!

You do not treat your friends like this, you do not speak to them like this and you do not treat your boss, kids, partner or family like this. Or maybe you do, maybe the hatred can no longer be contained and is now leaking out towards those you care about. You don't like it. You open your mouth and couldn't be more surprised at what might slip out. It's not you, and it's not who you are. It just makes you more frustrated and even more judgemental of yourself and others.

Self-hatred lives in the subconscious. Most of us never realise the depths of it, or the enormity of it. Self-hatred in even its mildest form prevents joy from ever capturing your soul and singing from the pure pleasure of being and having.

When you connect with that joy, it just feels like ecstasy, unlike anything that you've experienced before. As I sit writing this, my joy that you are hearing such a possibility brings me to tears in the hope that this too will become you. I used to hate me worse than anything or anyone else, and worse, I didn't understand that I did.

One day, I heard my five-year-old daughter using my words and I was taken aback at the nastiness of it. I immediately told her off for being so mean to herself. She looked at me defiantly and said, "Well you do it, you say the exact same thing!"

It was such an eye-opener to see that I actually didn't like who I was or how I was.

The more I looked, the more I didn't like, and I felt such despair at how I would ever get rid of it. It was like a parasite. It had leached into every part of me and was taking away the brilliance and the love and the joy that was intrinsically *me*.

So, I began the journey of discovering my self-love by finding and eliminating the hatred.

That's exactly what we're going to do with you!

Then you'll be able to let self-love have its way with you, each and every day. I feel happy when I wake up, no matter what has happened the day before and what is happening in my life. I know hope and joy is my everyday companion. I never really knew happiness before, never imagined that it could really be this good outside of the movies!

Self-hatred is such a harsh term, and I'm sure you may even feel that you're not that bad. I certainly didn't think I was that bad at all, but to see it from the outside in a little girl who was just mirroring what she'd learned from her mum was heart-breaking.

You'll just have to trust me for now that if you've been drawn to this book, you carry enough lack of self-love within to make a difference. It doesn't matter how we term it, you have so much more that you could be experiencing in your life to bring you joy and love. My job is to help you achieve that. There's nothing more thrilling than not recognising someone in the street who has changed and evolved so much from when you first met them.

Self-hatred needs to be healed to bring in love, joy and abundance. So where does it stem from and how does it have so much power over us? We talked a lot in chapter eight about the triggers that create the potential for a lack of self-love and they are quite eye-opening. Somewhere along the line we have come up with the perfect recipe to destroy our behaviour patterning which creates self-love. The brain begins reprogramming itself from its natural state of appreciation and love for the self into a more negative framework which becomes critical.

No longer is your body able to direct its natural love energy towards the self. It now points outwards. What the body learns very quickly is that if it can't receive its own love, the type that will fuel our self-worth and self-esteem, it will source it from those around you. Now you're in a situation where you need others to make you feel loved!

A human's natural state is to feed that need for love from within ourselves. When you've experienced the perfect combination of the triggers we discussed earlier, you become unable to do this. So, where as a child do you find the love? You turn to those around you of course; parents, siblings, grandparents, family and friends and because you're young, you're still cute enough to receive their attention. One day, you get a bit more attention than you need and it creates a window of opportunity. Like metal filaments to a magnet, or moths to a light, you start to gravitate toward getting more of that love and/or attention from others and re-shaping your behaviour. Perhaps you become extra cute, extra kind or giving or helpful, extra funny, or as a last resort, you become needy or naughty.

And there you have it! You think you have the perfect ingredients for success in love ... although it's not really success. You have worked out how to fill or fuel your hunger for love from others, but you have not yet realised that it is the self-love deficit you should be filling. You may not ever realise.

One day, there'll be a time where you might come to the realisation that you could love yourself more. Perhaps you're happy enough with how you are, perhaps you've been taught to be happy with whatever you've been given in life. But perhaps your hunger for change, or more of what you know now, will be greater than your fear of change and entering the unknown. I hope that day is today. If not, you can always come back to it.

I've created a meditation to heal the self-hatred in you, so that you can have another chance ...

✓ to love yourself

✓ to be truly happy

✓ to feed you own needs

✓ to drop away the neediness of others

✓ to be more fun to be around

✓ to be flexible and open to new opportunities

Let's get meditating and make this happen.

Meditation:
Deleting the Self-Hatred

Do this meditation every day for seven days, then at least once a week.

Read or speak it slowly, with pauses at the end of sentences. Take yourself to a quiet space where you'll not be interrupted for a while. Turn off your phone, close the door and get yourself comfortable.

It's time to breathe, to let go.

We're going to help the body to release all that it is holding within that is creating any feelings or self-hatred.

Or loving yourself less than you deserve.

As you breathe, you are slowing each breath.

In through the nose ... out through the mouth.

There's a sense of silence that is settling over you.

Each and every breath is making you more and more relaxed.

As you breathe you feel your breath almost passing through the confines of your lungs.

It's almost as if you can breathe anywhere in the body.

Breathing slower and slower ... your body knows now that it is safe.

Each and every breath makes you feel even safer.

As you breathe, you find your breath is naturally going into the heart.

Your heart responds with such joy and peace with each and every breath.

You can feel your internal intelligence and wisdom being awakened.

As your body is dropping into peace.

Your body is beginning to really relax and is becoming heavier in your chair or where you're lying.

There is so much to heal.

You have been living the hurts of the past.

They have been colouring your ability to live in the now.

To see what is really true for you.

You are breathing into any fear that might be rising in response to the idea of going back into those past pains.

You can relax, I've made it easy for you, you don't have to worry.

Imagine yourself to be in a hugely enormous protective bubble of golden light.

This bubble will prevent you from having more pain of this experience lodging in your body.

You have become the victim of past hurts.

Past relationships and past failures.

You believe yourself to be less than you truly are.

You can hardly stomach or believe my words.

They feel so foreign to you.

Yes, dear one, you are enough.

You are worthy of being loved.

You are more than you suppose.

You feel waves of anger, or irritation, or despair, or disgust ... all at the thought of you.

Then impatience at the thought that it could ever be better for you.

Yet you breathe ever so deeply into every emotion, as it rises up.

It's disappearing and dissolving away with every breath.

You seek the part in your body that is calling to you, perhaps it is in pain.

Perhaps it feels darker than the rest or your body.

Or perhaps it feels empty or lost.

You imagine you can be small enough and magical enough to see inside this area of your body.

You realise that there's a memory rising.

You feel your protective bubble and you know that you're safe.

That all is well in your world.

That this is simply a part of you that wishes to be freed.

You might see a person or people or a situation from the past or maybe even all of them together.

You are distant from this experience.

It is like you are watching it on a movie screen.

In fact, that's just what it looks like.

You find you can watch with the wisdom of a master or a sage.

And that you can see more than you could see when this situation was real to you.

You see the emotions and feel them, yet they have no pain in them.

You feel the sadness and the anger and the abandonment and

the betrayal and they disintegrate the very moment you begin to feel them.

You relax ... this is not scary at all...

The internal wisdom of the body is healing you as it releases.

You realise that you've been releasing old hurts and pains the whole time you've been here.

They just don't feel like they hurt you anymore.

There is no power for this person or circumstance to hurt you anymore.

If you truly let it all go.

You so want to let it go, to be free of it and to be happy.

You find yourself forgiving them all for the purpose of your own freedom.

This has no power over you anymore.

It comes naturally and freely.

And then you see the true magic of what has been happening.

As you breathe, every single breath is making your body like the red sands of a desert.

The winds of that desert are shifting through you and as they shift.

You can feel your body melding and moulding to a new way of being.

The heart has been challenging the hold of the feelings of hatred within.

And the feelings of unforgiveness that you've buried inside.

You feel a willingness to let them go and become aware of two areas in your pelvis.

Somewhere between your hips you have buried those feelings of self-hatred and they have become ever so tight for you.

These little balls have become buried down low, hiding behind the ovaries if you're female.

Or a bit lower if you're male.

You feel so relieved to have found them.

They have been hurting you for ever so long.

You're breathing even deeper now.

And the reddened sands within you are shifting in response.

The tightness in these balls is loosening and letting go.

Bit by bit with each and every breath.

You breathe even deeper and feel waves of love sourcing from your heart.

Flooding your body in response.

The balls are gone for now.

You are free from the hatred you gathered at that time.

You understand as you experience the waves of the heart love through the body, that you can find proof of anything ... if you are looking for it.

You know now that what you thought was not always true.

You understand that you were learning.

You weren't a failure at all.

The waves of love are feeding your body and you feel such love and joy and ...

What *is* that?

Wow ... you're feeling enough ... you're feeling like you're worthy.

Releasing the hatred is allowing room for these feelings of worth to arise.

Such joy and relief flood through your body.

You are on your way back to you.

You take time to sit in those feelings.

The room and its noises float back into your awareness and you are once again feeling solid again.

You imagine your energy coursing through your body and you can feel it tingling inside you.

You feel the connection of the Earth beneath you, anchoring you once again into your physicality and gently open your eyes.

As you drink some water, you adjust to this new way of feeling.

You know things are going to change and you feel so excited for the change.

You rise slowly when you're ready or snuggle down to sleep.

Recovery

Sleeping six hours straight in my own bed creates an incredible bliss, especially upon waking up in my own home. I did wake on and off in the early parts of the night, yet each time the familiar sounds of home and the snoring of the dog would lull me back into a deep state of rest. Being home amid such familiarity is reassuring, as I begin the recovery from three weeks of severe sleep deprivation. It feels good. When I wake, it is to Berni smiling and gazing at me. He's always had this thing that he calls 'Karina gazing', where he is overcome with feelings of love for me. He just stares at me until I see him, loving the freedom of watching what he sees as the beauty in me, entirely unnoticed.

He tells me to relax and snooze while he does school drop off. I need no encouragement and snuggle down under the lightness of the doona. Next time I wake, he is holding a turmeric soy chai latte from my favourite ultra-healthy cafe and a mango smoothie. I think if I didn't already love him, I might just fall in love with him in this very moment. He looks like an angel with those drinks in his hands! For the better part of three weeks I have not been able to eat or drink at all. I miss my fresh chai latte like coffee lovers would be missing their coffee!

This particular moment is etched into my memory, although it is a pattern that Berni will repeat each morning. Fuelling me with good foods is his next biggest challenge, as he isn't a cook. Luckily the fridge and freezer are still full. The school mums are still bringing food and have been very generous with their catering!

Bern has been so much to me during this journey. After finishing my first shower at home, I see myself for the first time in the full-length mirror. I realise just how protected I have been from the extent of my scar. Tiny hospital bathroom mirrors could not show me just what being cut from my breasts to my pubic line really looked like.

I'm standing there naked; so bare and so skinny and so broken.

The scar is enormous, long and dark red with multiple bulges which had obviously occurred during the violent vomiting. Tears fall down my face, and then *he's* there behind me, holding me and telling me I'm beautiful. He stops me as I shake my head and try to speak.

"I love this scar. This is your life-line. It reminds me every day of just how precious you are, and how lucky I am to still have you," Berni tells me. "This is proof that you have survived. Love your scar as much as I love you, it's as much a part of you as anything else."

I hear his words and hate them. I don't want cancer to be a part of me.

Maddie is packing up her room and taking carloads of stuff at a time to her new place. Her last day at home is Friday, when Berni packs her furniture and remaining boxes into the van. She's so excited and I'm really excited for her, although there's a little pang when she's gone and I'm left in the house on my own. It seems very lonely and way too silent. I think back to the excitement and freedom I felt on moving out of home and my heart sings for her.

You'd think as she's the third child to move out that it wouldn't matter, yet there's a pain in my heart at the thought of losing her. I shake it off; she's not lost and I know exactly where she is. We take a trip over the weekend to buy new sofas and plan to turn her room into a music room and retreat. The furniture is beautiful and we're just hoping it will arrive before the party we're planning.

Two furniture stores and I'm exhausted, where has my stamina gone?

It seems that my first week home passes in a blur of sleeping on and off. I have the residue of so many drugs in my system to clear and so much sleep to recover. The trauma of what my body and I have been through has taken its toll. I'm very skinny compared to when I was admitted. I'm happy with my new weight, yet David wants me to focus on putting the weight back on for now to give my body the fuel to heal.

We see him a week after I go home to discuss the pathology findings of the tumour, as I've been way too sick while in hospital. He has that grim look on his face as he tells me that my cancer is an aggressive form of liposarcoma, the same type given as the diagnosis on the original scan. He talks percentages as doctors do and my eyes glaze over, as I feel the fear rising. He suggests that it wouldn't hurt to talk to the oncologists about treatment options, despite having told me in the beginning that chemotherapy doesn't work for this cancer. We're a bit confused and agree to at least talk to them. I'm free to call the medical rooms anytime I need to, otherwise I'll see him in three months' time.

As we get into the car, Berni looks at my face and I feel like I'm going to fall apart. The odds I've been given aren't terrible but they aren't great. The first thing he says is the perfect thing I need to hear, and I want to kiss him in gratitude.

"They are not your odds. They are not your percentages. They relate to other people with cancer who may not have had the benefit of the incredible healing you do. Even if they were, there is the percentage that survived, so why shouldn't that be you? That is the medical profession's best estimate based on past performance. You are not any of those patients. You are you and you carry your own destiny and your odds are based upon that. I'm betting you survive without another trace of cancer. I just can't see you getting it back ever again."

I just love this man.

He is my ideal match. He balances me perfectly, and we are rarely in fear at the same time. He's much more grounded than I am. As I look into his eyes, my own faith returns and I am blessed with this huge wave of peace washing through my body.

He has his moments and it takes him a week to break down, as he realises that we've made it. He's been looking at me as if I am the most precious piece of gold and possibly about to break at any moment. He's overprotective and super loving. I couldn't be luckier to be doing this journey with a man who loves me so much. Tears of gratitude for his love, acceptance and support come and go those first weeks.

Having spent the better part of seven weeks taking mostly unexpected leave, the backlog in Berni's workload is becoming apparent. He has been working to do the essentials each day, but that's all he's been up to. He's so drawn, he wants to be with me, but I know he needs to go back to work. He's had incredible support from the Australian management of his firm who have stood up to the pressure coming from the international management overseas. I tell him that I don't want him to go back to work, but I think it's time. I've got heaps of offers from people who wish to look after me, those who can help at a moment's notice, so I think I'll be okay. I think that the quiet will do me good.

When he says that he doesn't want to go back to work, I misunderstand and tell him I don't want him to go back either. He looks at me and says the words I thought I'd never hear. "I don't think you understand, I don't want to go back to working there. This has changed me. Life is too short to live with that kind of pressure and difficulty forever."

We talk about it for a long time. His workplace culture has changed following an international takeover some months before. Communication was made difficult with the language and cultural barriers, creating frustration, no doubt, on both sides. I'd watched Bern go from loving work and thriving on the challenges it provided, to dragging himself there. Long hours had always been a part of his role, but prior to my illness, they'd always been manageable in the long term, because he loved what he did. Now we are looking at a life that has been forever changed. I suggest we manifest a situation where he can leave and be paid out to go. Financially it would be great, and he'd have the chance to choose a role that would once again make his heart sing.

Life is short and you only get one chance to live each day before it's gone.

A couple of weeks later it's our wedding anniversary, and this year it's particularly poignant celebrating at our favourite restaurant. We reflect upon our amazing trip to Paris the year before to renew our vows and what a blessing it is to be here, able to celebrate. Everything in life has gained so much more meaning. We are taking our chances and planning to live life to the full. Every decision seems to have so much more meaning.

After walking away from the doctor with a referral for an oncologist, I slide into the biggest depression for three days. This is the worst I've felt since the hospital—I'm nauseous all the time and my body no longer feels like mine.

It occurs to me while talking to a friend that I am wasting my time, and subsequently, that of the oncologist. I have no intention of having chemotherapy on a cancer that is not currently in my body, especially when it's efficacy is unclear. As soon as I remember myself and what intuitively feels right, I cancel the appointment. I know that if I ignore my intuition one more time, I would only hate myself more. The last time I ignored my intuition, it gave the tumour time to grow. I don't want to repeat the same patterns of self-criticism that stem from ignoring what I know so deeply inside.

Berni reluctantly drags himself back to work, and I've been given the green light to drive whenever I feel ready. I have my freedom back, yet everything is feeling so different. I am so tired all the time, and am suffering an excruciating vulnerability at feeling so broken. I am carrying the trauma of the hospital;

jumping at noises and feeling so tender inside. My physical wounds are healing, yet my emotional wounds are struggling to let go. I'm still dealing with the trauma of everything that has happened to me. These wounds feel too raw to face them in order to let them go. Every time I looked at people, they look at me with care, concern or sympathy. I feel so blessed that I have so much care around me, yet the rawness of my soul remains.

I have flashbacks of the hospital and the terrible events there. I can't even face a green smoothie without remembering the green fluid that was my daily companion in vomit bags and tubes for weeks. I'm trying to recover my strength to go back to work.

I'm spending lots of time sleeping, and taking time to recover the things that make my heart sing. Looking for the sources of my joy and working with them is helping too. I'm seeing the healers at Flying Souls Institute of Healing to fast-track the healing of the hospital trauma. While I might be having difficulty in facing things myself, the fabulous thing about Meliae Intuitive Healing is that the healers can support you to do just that. It's mostly painless and you can fast-track through the hard stuff. I'm not comfortable suffering, so I choose to heal anything that causes me pain as soon as I can manage it.

I'm not able to go back to training yet, but walking our little dog is very therapeutic. Right now, the sunshine and the fresh air from the ocean combine to revive my self-confidence. I'm not healing anyone else yet, but my ability to heal has returned bigger, faster and stronger than anything I'd ever imagined possible. I've always been fast, yet now I can heal in ten minutes something which might have taken an hour before.

I toy with the idea of when to go back to work while I work on healing myself. I have to be in good shape emotionally, as well as physically, and I'm motivated to heal the whole cancer and hospital experience. The trauma of my stay was significant and it takes a lot of time and energy to heal what is present for me.

Having counselled cancer patients as they leave hospital, I know that you're never really free of cancer. That knowledge is becoming my reality, as every twang or twinge or pain takes me into moments of fear. I contemplate everything I feel as a potential new tumour.

I curse medicine for it's way of thinking and managing cancer survivors.

Giving someone odds in their way does not empower the patient to focus on being positive and create the energy and drive to live. I believe that attitude is everything and even I'm struggling.

Why, oh why can they not focus on the positive?

"You have this % chance of living" fosters a way more positive attitude, rather than always having your predicted % chance of dying in the back of your mind.

Recuperating gives me so much time to myself. I have a pile of books to read, and as this is something that I never manage to make time for, I am one happy girl. I watch the styles of writing as I read, always looking at how best to engage the reader.

I organise replacing the carpet in our new retreat due to a hole in the centre of the floor from an electrical point. My carpet in the office also gets replaced due to damage from the previous owners. I managed to find carpet and installation that can be done in time for the party.

Yes, we're having a party!

We've been so overwhelmed by the help, love, care and offers from so many people around us that we've reason to celebrate. We want to say thank you.

As we finish the list of invitees, we cannot believe just how many people are on it. We check and double check and find we'll be having a party for over two hundred people! Our house is, by definition, a perfect party house, so we can fit the numbers. Given our fondness for gathering people together, accommodating parties was a must-have on our house-hunting wish list.

I'm now busy organising caterers, glasses and a dress for our special event, nicknamed 'Bye-bye Tessie', a 'celebrating life' party. We decided to give the tumour a name when I decided that Berni's nickname for it was not suitable for show and tell at Zavier's school. Talking to a nine-year-old about Tessie the Tumour is a lot less scary than calling it cancer, so Tessie it became.

And finally, I'm back at work, after what seems like forever.

Initially, my very short hours help me to deal with the toll healing is taking upon my body. I'm a lot more tired than I used to be after a day's healing. I can barely tell if it is due to my recovery or the fact that my ability to heal is now incredibly powerful. I am doing so much more healing in a day than I have previously, and my days are half the size! Each day I go home to rest before school pickup, so I'm very mindful of creating new habits to support my body.

We decide I'm fine to work, as long as I'm looking after me.

That means I can do healing or look after the home, but definitely not both. The combination of having to do shopping, cooking, washing and tidying, along with the normal requirements for running our family are just too much. Berni is still helping as much as he can, but he's under a lot of pressure to catch up at work.

I fall into bed in tears most nights. The tiredness is too much. Maddie isn't living here and Lachy's doing the run up to his final exams of his schooling. I am so mindful that my journey of cancer has already wreaked havoc on his studies and cannot bring myself to ask him to help unless I'm desperate.

As each day passes, it improves, and I've blocked out some time here and there for greater breaks. I'm teaching evening meditation classes, but that's getting hard, being so late. We've found a new teacher and healer to take over my night class, and I swap to the morning class. I'm creating more balance, yet each day is a challenge to evaluate just exactly what is out of balance, and how to fix or work around it. Sleep is still a challenge.

Berni is working harder than ever and there's so much stress at work. No one looks happy there anymore. He works into the night regularly, either disturbing me when he comes to bed or I stay up until I'm exhausted, just for the company. It's like I'm seeing the limits of my body for the first time and I'm devastated to realise just how far I have been pushing it past its limits for decades. I literally have had nothing in the tank for years.

No wonder my immunity didn't kick in to fight the cancer!

I find the most perfect dress and shoes to match for the party, and have even managed to organise to have my family come from Queensland to join us. My mother is making a second trip to Melbourne from the country and they're all staying in a holiday house I've organised for the weekend. Dad's not coming, but that's not surprising. He hates Melbourne and has a back problem that makes long trips difficult for him. We're all disappointed, as it would have meant my whole family was together for the first time since my grandfather's funeral, eleven years ago. Still, it looks like being an awesome party, with one hundred and thirty people expected. I'm not sure I'd have managed if everyone had been able to make it!

The hair and makeup artist leaves only minutes before the guests start arriving. Thankfully, no one is on time! Alesa and Denise have helped with the setup earlier, so everything is ready. All day I have been feeling very emotional. Alesa had given me some healing to help me manage. I am so worried as to how I am going to cope tonight. For so many it is the first time they've seen me since I was diagnosed or in hospital.

I want to spend the night celebrating my recovery, not talking about the cancer. We decide on having early speeches so that I can just say it all once and then focus on having fun.

There is a constant stream of people entering through the front door. The security guards at the gate seem to be managing to slow down the flow so I can properly greet everyone. Without exception, everyone is so happy and cannot believe how great

I'm looking. As I catch sight of myself in the mirror, I'm forced to agree. Despite the instant appeal of the hair and makeup, I'm glowing with health and happiness. My eyes are sparkling and I'm swishing the skirt of my designer dress around as I beam with joy. There are presents and hugs and tears everywhere. Berni is beaming and everyone is so, so happy. As planned, the speeches begin early with the DJ calling the crowd inside.

Berni and I gather Dylan, Lachy and Zavier up the front. Elyse is away for work and Maddie will be coming a bit later due to a concert she'd already booked tickets to. We feel a bit lopsided without the girls, yet that disappears as I take the microphone.

I stand there, grateful for its weight, as I use it to steady me. As I focus on slowing my breathing, I see healing hands turning towards me and love projecting forward from hundreds of eyes. I go to speak but find that for once, I seem lost for words. I love to talk, so this has happened very rarely in my life. I think Berni's proposal was the last time I was speechless!

I eventually find my voice and I speak from my heart to theirs, thanking them all for the myriad of ways in which they have helped Berni, the children, and of course, me. I thank them for their messages, visits, calls, emails, healing, meals, flowers, gifts and the positive energy that everyone has rallied to give. "I feel like I've been looking down the barrel of a gun and just dodged its most vicious bullet."

I talk of my healing journey and of where I'm at right now. I tell them how humbling and traumatic these last months have been for us all. I speak of the importance of love and family and of each of them there. I encourage them to hold close those they love, and to never waste a minute.

I speak of my joy, of how lucky I am to have such incredible kids and of the contributions they've each made. Then I speak of Berni and my love for him, of his support and his love for me, and very soon there's barely a dry eye in the place. My eyes blur as the emotion takes over.

I really can't believe that I am actually here!

I tell them that with so many gathered around, it's like I'm looking at the wake of my funeral, yet I'm here and I'm alive.

I'm truly the luckiest girl in the world.

I tell them that as I'm alive, I plan to celebrate. "See you on the dance floor!"

Berni takes the microphone and speaks of his great love for our children and their support, and of his enormous gratitude of everyone here. He tells them all that he could never have done it without them. He speaks of the value of life, the error of putting work before family, and of his altered perspective and priorities. Then he speaks of the great love he has for me, and the person I am, and the tears are flowing everywhere. I wish for a moment we'd put out boxes of tissues. He too is overwhelmed with emotion, and his hugs and kisses for me are echoed over and over.

The DJ ups the volume of the music and we are dancing. I'm joined by so many people with whom I've danced with over the years, and who share my gratitude that I'm well enough to dance again. I let the music take me, feeling its rhythm and allowing my body to be free in its movement. Mum is sitting on the couch nearby and she looks the happiest I've ever seen her. In fact, everyone looks so happy and I am taken with the joy that is now pumping through the room.

I remember the darkest times in the hospital and how I took myself into the future, to this exact moment on the dance floor. And then the hospital is gone and I'm just in the joy of the moment.

I'm healthy and I'm well and I'm cancer free!

I'm singing at the top of my voice which is drowned out by the music. I'm dancing and singing and I'm happy. I'm spinning around and around, faster and faster. The skirt of my dress is spinning outwards in response and I'm lost in the joy of being alive and surrounded by those I love.

I'm so very happy.

Fear vs. Love

When Berni fell in love with me, I'm not sure he realised what he was in for. He'll argue and say the love that I give to both he and his children, and all that I have brought to his life, has been well worth it. He's a very generous man, for he found himself with a very broken bird. My journey pre-Berni had been rocky, to say the least. I had left a marriage and was seen as a terrible mother who was putting her children through the trauma of divorce for my own selfish needs.

I didn't quite see it that way.

I looked at our marriage and hated it, every single bit of it. My desire to give my children a proper family that included a father was the only reason I stayed so long. Fifteen years was a long time to be unhappy a lot of the time. At first, I was unhappy because he didn't want to just get engaged and married like normal people do. I believed that you should love someone so much that you didn't want to live away from them.

He said that only happened in fairytales.

It was clear to me that he didn't love me enough to want me forever, which had me feeling angry and entirely unloved. We decided a month's break would allow him time to gain perspective as to how he felt about getting so serious in just a couple of years.

I found out I was pregnant two days after we broke up. Unwilling to make the pregnancy his reason to stay with me, I kept it to myself. Two weeks later, I was standing in the hospital bathroom in my nursing uniform with blood pouring down my legs.

I had lost the baby.

The pain was too much. I had no one I could tell and the ward was too busy with critically ill patients for me to be able to go home. So, I cleaned myself up and inched through the day. When he called two days later saying he'd made a mistake, that he missed me and wanted me back, I was too sad to decide any differently. I was desperate for someone to hold me and take the pain away.

Everyone was continually asking him when he was going to propose, and a year later we decided to move in together. Actually, he decided he had to live with me first, to try me out. He said that he never wanted to hurt me like his father had hurt his mother, and I relented.

At the time, I was very much against living together before marriage. Moving in with him went against everything that was important to me, and was a humiliation. I wanted him to sweep me off my feet with his love, but that clearly wasn't the kind of love he had for me.

My intuition was screaming at me to break up for good, but I was too scared to listen. I didn't want to contemplate a life of being alone. I already believed no one else would love me. I couldn't see my own worth, so I started to ignore the loving and supportive voice that was my intuition. I tried never to listen and would push away anything that suggested I would have a wonderful life on my own. My intuition was well on its way to shutting down.

The day I agreed to move in was the first day I began to give away what defined me, and that which made my heart sing. I was so desperate to be loved that I would have agreed to anything.

People looked at me in sympathy when we told them about our living arrangements. Back then, there was so much social stigma about living together—it was still called 'living in sin'. My grandmother wasn't dead, but it was as if she was rolling over in her future grave in horror at my news. I was so ashamed and sorry to disappoint her. I felt so lonely at a time when I should have had so much joy. I knew without doubt that he was not the heart that was meant to love me. But who was I to be choosy? I wore glasses and had a crooked and protruding tooth. I wasn't the greatest catch and he made me feel safe.

Our marriage went a lot like that. We'd have an argument about something he didn't like in me, and to keep the peace I would relent and put it away. Bit by bit I was losing my colour—my brilliance was dimming by the day. I didn't love myself enough to see that I deserved to be the essence that was me. My confidence ebbed away and I began to refer every choice to him for approval. Later on, I couldn't even change our brand of nappies without first getting his okay.

Eventually, I got my fairytale wedding and looked like a princess. Surely now we were married, life would be perfect? My belief that no one else would love me continued throughout our marriage, despite straightening my teeth and getting contact lenses. We did all the things young couples do. We saved hard and built a house together, and on the surface, things probably looked okay.

In time, I created an unlikely alliance with a couple of girls he worked with. I met them at corporate social events, and I thought they liked me, yet they would give him odd looks. Often, this happened when he played out his habit of putting me down or teasing me in front of others. He'd comment to his colleagues and even his clients about my small breasts at every occasion. "More than a mouthful is a waste," he'd laugh, thinking he was being entertaining.

It was excruciating to me.

I couldn't be more embarrassed having these strangers assessing my tits, or lack of them. I assumed their uncomfortable laughs were aimed at my inadequacy, rather than embarrassment that I was being treated this way. After what happened to me as a child, I was particularly shy about such matters with strangers. I was still haunted by the need to hide my breasts, and having them showcased so negatively was like acid to my soul. My self-confidence slid away and I couldn't imagine that anyone else would love or want me, so I stayed.

The girls were very protective of me, and I would find out years later, speaking to a couple of his female colleagues, that this was because I was so nice and he was so arrogant. They saw us as such a mismatched couple, and they hated his constant jokes at my expense.

I had been told I wouldn't have children naturally due to endometriosis, so I was very surprised to find myself pregnant. The birth of Maddie changed me and gave me the most beautiful little girl to distract me from the deteriorating state of our marriage. I filled our house with friends and other young families to colour my world with distraction. By the time I was pregnant with Lachy, I knew my marriage was well and truly over, but here I was, about to be a mother to two young children, so I tried to make the best of things. I was too frightened to become a single mum. How would I ever cope financially with two small children, especially without any family in a position to help me?

Life went on and I got lonelier and lonelier. My husband completed his postgraduate studies and spent time travelling for work. I loved the silence and the time out it gave me. We built a bigger house and soon I could no longer ignore what I was living. Heavy drinking and socialising was a big part of his industry and it didn't do our marriage any favours.

He was heavily critical when things went wrong; everything seemed to be my fault. While I believed what he said on the inside, I was trying hard to prove him wrong. It meant we were arguing all the time. We couldn't seem to see eye to eye on anything.

He was working to support the family and I was working part-time night duty as a nurse to increase our payments on the mortgage. I worked hard both physically and mentally in a busy high dependency surgical ward, and the toll taken on my body working nights was huge. I lost half a night's sleep every week to minimise the amount of time the children were spending in childcare. I felt and looked like I was aging prematurely by the day. As I was working part-time, most of the housework and running of the family fell to me. I was exhausted and not feeling heard when I voiced that I was struggling. I felt so depressed.

My fear of raising the children alone was finally overtaken by my inability to live like this anymore. I couldn't take my misery any longer. Our 'talks' every few months to discuss my misery were going nowhere. I wanted to leave, but once again was persuaded to give the marriage and him another chance. Changes were made, yet it would be a chance conversation that would turn everything around.

My close friend Kathryn had caught up with an old friend of hers who was now doing reiki and teaching meditation classes. I was persuaded by her enthusiasm and assurance that this was something I had to try. Danni and her reiki, followed by her meditation classes, actually saved me. She gave me a tool to lift away my misery, to start seeing myself and to reconnect with my intuition.

Once it was reconnected, I started to fly.

I did a tarot reading weekend workshop and found myself again. A new healer, Ida, took over my healings and created significant release for me, expanding on the work Danni had begun. I had never been happier and under her tutelage I trained as a healer.

Healing meant that I worked on letting go of a lot of what I hated about myself. I worked on my confidence and found my joy once I began to live intuitively again. When I talked to others, I seemed happier than I'd ever been and I'd tell them so, but I was omitting the lack of love and passion in my life, and the conflict in my marriage. I was much happier, as I changed how I was interacting with him and my world. I felt much more empowered, but in reality, I was very lonely.

Word started to spread of my ability to read auras, energy and to heal others. Soon I was inundated with clients and then I started teaching meditation. I faced my fear when my love for this work became more important than the fear of standing up to him and leaving my job as nurse.

Interestingly, I never had a fear that I wouldn't make it. The ability to work casual shifts at high agency rates meant that I had a backup if I needed it to pay the mortgage. He let me resign, although by then it wasn't really a choice. I was following my heart and doing it regardless. It was simply a question of whether he would be coming along for the ride.

One day we had an argument that broke our marriage for good. It wasn't even that big a deal. I had purchased a paper shredder to adhere to the new privacy laws for my growing spiritual and healing business. He reacted aggressively to the news that I would spend $100 on something so 'stupid' and 'frivolous' when that money could be decreasing our mortgage.

I don't know what happened in that moment, but something snapped in me.

He hadn't hit me, but he had effectively broken the hold that fear had over me. At that moment, I knew that being alone could never be as lonely as living with someone you couldn't reach. I did love him, but only enough to leave before I really started to hate him. I knew it would be harder for our children if we couldn't get along.

I did not want Maddie growing up thinking that her parents' marriage was an example of the best she could hope for in love. I wanted more for her. I didn't want Lachy growing up thinking that this was how you treated the woman that you supposedly loved. I wanted more for him too.

I wanted to be happy and I knew I deserved a chance at love, and I still cared enough about him to know that he did too.

I could see clearly now.

We were not the right recipe for each other. We had turned each other into people we didn't want to be. I certainly didn't like the woman I had become, and that dislike had created the compulsion to heal, thinking that if I healed everything in me that he complained about, it would fix our marriage.

In a way, it fixed it completely!

What healing did was show me that there wasn't anything wrong with me.

I did have behaviours, beliefs and attitudes that were not working for me, and were even, on occasion, destructive, but that did not make me 'not enough'. I started to see who I was through the eyes of others, and I liked what I saw. I was not what I had believed myself to be.

Love had won the war with fear. I finally loved myself enough to leave, knowing that divorce would have both negative and positive ramifications on my children. Surely having two happy parents would be a better life than living each day with parents in constant conflict and fighting?

Action!
Dissolving the Power of
the Past to Hurt You

When I think about the past, I think about how lucky I am to have come out unscathed after so many incredibly challenging events. Many people around me would have been unaware that I was in so much pain, that I was suffering from depression, and that I lived in so much fear. If anything, they'd have seen the opposite, and a good deal of that goes back to my childhood.

My family have always been very private, living by the premise of 'what's happening at home, stays at home'. It was a common ethos in those days, but it was something that I grew to hate. My first marriage had the same rules, which is the worst thing possible. To feel unable to share with friends or advisers when you are struggling and needing help is damaging. Feeling alone and isolated compounded my struggle and amplified my depression. When I was out of ideas on how to cope, I had no one to turn to. Back then, I imagine it was a protective cloak from adverse judgement within the community.

For me, it was like having a noose around my neck.

I am what I call an *internaliser*, someone who bottles up the pain or sadness or anger or the emotions that hurt, instead of expressing them out loud. I did it to keep the peace, to protect someone's feelings, or to prevent others from seeing my pain. I was too embarrassed to allow others to think I wasn't doing as well as I should be doing, and so I kept my humiliation firmly on the inside. It's not the greatest way to live as that negative emotion becomes like an acid to the body.

I'm sure this played a big part in my getting cancer.

My family are still quite private to varying degrees. My sister was only just asking me the other day about the contents of this book and its possible ramifications. No one lives a perfect life; we all make mistakes and don't do things as well as we could or would have liked. None of us wants others thinking we've failed or are not good enough. There will be people who would prefer they weren't in this book, yet my story must be told. I did not survive cancer for no reason. I don't want to keep it private on the inside anymore.

It has hurt me for long enough.

I'm not writing this book to make others look bad. I had my part in every event and I'm just as likely to be judged harshly as with compassion. I'm hoping my story will prevent others from repeating *their* version of my experience.

How I interpreted my experiences as I evolved through life led me to hate who I was. It wasn't until I was thirty that I began to see things differently. All of a sudden, I knew I didn't want to carry this pain anymore, I'd had enough of being so sad.

We all carry a story. We carry stories about every situation in our past. Our stories tell us who we are and define our passage forward.

But what if those stories (or at least some of them) are not actually true?

As we live an event, we interpret it through the looking glasses of the pain and joy of what we have experienced in the past. If you were to create a story that told you that you were a failure, every experience going forward will have the ability to prove you to be that failure. Yet it also has the ability to prove that you're not, although in reality, it's likely that past experiences will colour your vision in a negative way. It's very much like looking at a glass that has been filled exactly halfway. Depending upon your perspective and your past, the glass is either half full or half empty.

I used to be the glass half empty type of girl. My fear drove me to look for what was missing, what could go wrong, and thus I learned how to control negative outcomes. I found that if I planned everything, a lot less could go wrong. Alas, by the same token, little could surprise me. When you're conducting risk management with fear daily, it destroys the capacity for surprise and spontaneity, and therefore joy. Your life is less for it.

So how do you get to the glass half full? Luckily, you are already working with your fear, and this will make more of a difference than you can imagine. You can train your attitude to a whole new way of living, just through practice. In doing so, you will destroy that which gives fear the keys to divining your destiny.

This is what we'll do. We'll take away the power of the past to define or divine your future. You've already put your fear on notice, so next we will train your energy to be a magnet for this new way of living.

Here's a little mantra that speaks to the soul self and creates a clear platform to change your ability to be authentically the real you. Say it three times on waking, and as many times through the day as you can. The more you say it, the greater the magnetic pull for your success.

⌒

May it be,
May it be my daily joy,
May it be my ability to shine,
May it be my ability to love or be loved.

⌒

Next, we've got to change your way of interacting with your past.

The easiest way is to check your body. It interacts with your soul as a barometer to how you are travelling on this path. If your soul is fed, its needs met and is heard, your body and emotions will be in great shape. The body acts as the voice of the soul, a form of secondary feedback that tells you things have gone astray. The body speaks to you physically, when your primary means of communication is not effective. The soul needs you to listen for your journey to be one of ease and grace.

When you don't listen to the inner yearnings through which it communicates on a daily basis, it will react by creating pain or disease in your body to get your attention. So, when I have a problem in my body, I listen with full attention. I know that the body will tell me when I'm hating myself. It will either create the symptom or the opportunity for injury. Everything has a message to allow you to hear the tears of the soul when it has not been heard.

Your soul has never needed you like it needs you right now,
For your soul seeks for you to experience joy as your natural state.
It seeks for you to feel the experiences that you are creating,
To enable the learning of the soul.
It seeks for you to let go of any internalised or externalised hate,
That lives in the subconscious energy.
It seeks for you to experience and let go,
To forgive the pain and its cause and to move on.
You are not meant to suffer, to struggle, or to do it hard.
Seek the lesson in the experience and then it can go.

We're not supposed to hold the negativity in the experience within the body. I firmly believe that if you do, it will eventually create disease, and even cancer.

It's not always well received to be constantly right, yet your soul always is. It carries the higher wisdom and knowledge of your lifetimes of experience, and brings it forward as needed. You did not come here without a plan, or without help. You have sage advice that is available to you from your guides as well.

Most of us don't realise that we have angels and guides around us all the time who are trying to help us to do life more easily. I've never seen any person without at least eight primary and twenty secondary guides. It's like having the internet on tap. If I need to know something, I don't hesitate to google the answer. It's the same with my guides. I ask them for help when I'm stuck or just out of ideas. Why do things the hard way, when they're happy to help and guide you?

We each take away a different perspective from our experiences. It's part of the reason for us being here; to experiment, to create awareness through our feelings, of the brilliance of the love energy that underpins us all and everything around us. Ideally, we would approach each situation with the naivety and innocence of a child.

Have you watched them?

They let go and forgive so easily when they feel safe and loved. So really, that's what you need, to feel safe and loved. The mistake we make is to seek that love externally rather than from within. If we feed our own love, we will always be able to see the glass half full.

When we bask in the light of our own love, we live in possibility and hope. We are not seeing the lack, only that which we can create or solve, and the success that can be made. It's our natural state and our children do it so well, until life starts to get in the way, colouring their faith and their natural ability to make good in their lives. Once upon a time you were that child, so what we're doing is just returning you to your natural state. We don't have to invent or create it, it's just been lying dormant, awaiting a window of opportunity.

We need to heal. We need to let go. We need to be joyful and loving and loved. We want it, but how to create it? What will I have to give up to have this, and will it be worth it? You'll just have to take my word for it, every morning I wake up just like that, no matter what! I'm at peace with myself, my stories no longer have any power over me.

There's a hard way and a quick way to recreate that natural state within you, and of course, I was never going to publish this book until I'd mastered the quick way! The next chapter's guided meditation will help you achieve just that, and the other meditation tracks already have you on your way.

But before we get to that, we've got a bit of work to do. We need to discover how, where and why you're in the state you're in.

Healing the self

To heal the self, you first need to identify how its blockage is affecting you directly. Only then it is possible to clear it, and work the process of loving you. Finding its cause is easy if you have a Meliae Intuitive Healer at your disposal, but it does take time to work through the layers.

This book and its guided meditations will allow you the benefits of the equivalent of six months with a healer, by sharing pathways they use to identify, disempower and clear blocks. It's an empowering journey which allows you to truly own the brilliance that is you. The great news is that you don't have to slip into overwhelm, you have time to do this at your own pace. You don't have to do everything right now, just what needs to be done to make now easy.

Let's look at your body and its emotions to find the key as to where and how to heal. Listening to the body is a quick way to discern the cause/key to even the most deceptive or difficult problems. Listening to the mind is just as revealing. Stopping to listen can create a healing all of its own, while at the same time making short work of the healing you're trying to do.

We're looking for that which is resistant to change. Where can we find it and what can we do about it?

Once we identify what is lacking, we can work on letting go of the fear behind it (you already know how to master your fear) and then use easy, healthy, inexpensive and sensible ways to support your body better. Did it ever occur to you how hard your feet work to carry you, and just what your body deals with on a daily basis to allow you to learn the lessons you seek? Time to support it more effectively!

The Emotions

Become watchful. Notice everything ...

How am I reacting?

How am I feeling?

How am I behaving?

How do I treat me?

Emotion	Cause	Curative Action
Busy, Busy, Busy	Distraction, not listening to internal wisdom	Breathe and listen, give your soul the opportunity to be heard. Focus upon what is important in each situation. Let go of the drama.
Neediness	Lack of connection	Use the guided meditation in chapter 4 to connect. Find some earth/sand to put your bare feet on. Breathe until you feel your peace returning.
Over-caring	Ignoring the voice inside	Stop it! Breathe deeply. It isn't your job to do for and fix everyone else.
Punishment	Making you more wrong	Stop it! You are not to blame for everything. If you were, just start problem solving to fix it, or let it go.

Emotion	Cause	Curative Action
Sadness	Internalised pain of lack	Start looking for the lack in your life, once you've found it, feed it with healthy and empowered choices.
Sarcasm	Avoidance of your inner lack	If you find yourself here, retreat to quiet breathing to find what you don't like about you. Use the techniques you'll find later on in the book to address the lack.
Self-depreciation	Measuring your lack	You are not all bad. You are learning! Rather than beat yourself up, acknowledge that no one is good at everything, and that it is okay to be learning new things to make life easier. Just give yourself a break!

The Physical

Become watchful. Notice everything ...

How does my body feel?

What hurts?

What is not working or working too much?

Physical	Cause	Curative Action
Injury	Inattention to the urgings of the soul	Breathe and listen, give your soul the opportunity to be heard.
Lack of Correct Levels or Laxness in Structure	Not feeding the soul, not holding on to the joy	Does your body have enough good water, food, exercise, stimulation and rest? Create ways to fuel the body and to make joy an everyday experience.

Physical	Cause	Curative Action
Lack of Function e.g. underactive thyroid	No space to heal	When your soul is hurting, make time where you can use guided meditations to heal, or see a healer or therapist to work through the issues.
Over Function e.g. overactive thyroid	Compensation for your lack	This is a sign your soul is hurting due to some perceived lack of worth. Take time to work out what and to address the deficit. You are not as bad as you would have yourself think.
Tightness or Erosion of Muscles or Joints	Suppression of trauma or hurt	Take the time to feel your experiences, to drop into the emotion and let go. Use the guided meditations, a healer or a good therapist to work through old issues.
Tiredness & Lethargy	Exhaustion of the soul energy	Stop! Rest! Your body is in need. Look to the lack and address it. Ensure time for sleep and adequate rest.

Your soul is giving you messages all the time. You just need to listen. When you know where to find it, you can call for the message as to the physical or emotional problem. Of course, once you know what is missing, you can use the guided meditations to heal it and change your behaviours. It'll work on ensuring that you are paying attention in future. Then, because you already know what or where the problem is sourcing from, you can focus on creating new behaviours that support you better.

It's important to heal the pain of the past. If I hadn't, I would be unable to write this book or talk about my past without pain, humiliation and fear of judgement. The pain of the past is just that, something that belongs in the past, not driving you now. I know that if fear was still driving me, I'd be blaming someone for how I'm feeling and be lacking forgiveness.

I know some of you don't want to, or are not ready to forgive the past, and I don't blame you for it. Just remember that the only one carrying the pain will be you. Keeping yourself stuck in the past and judging yourself for your past performance, has the power to create a bucket load of physical or emotional ailments.

If you're wanting to punish someone for the pain of the past, you're wasting your time. Most people will and have moved on. I love that gorgeous quote from Oscar Wilde. *"Always forgive your enemies, nothing annoys them so much."*

Every time I think of it, it takes me out of my anger for a moment and I use it as a window into letting go and healing. Taking back your power is a natural result from the process of forgiveness. It's not the process of giving permission, or approval for behaviours that have hurt you, far from it. If it hurt you, then it was wrong for you. That's all that matters, and you can choose to walk forward, free of the pain, any time you like. You choose to let go and then all of a sudden, you've a heap of energy to use on making joy and fun and laughter. You start feeling better and hope starts sniffing around. Life starts getting good again.

There a lot of ways to get back into the driver's seat of your destiny. I use this recipe to create my success. It's easy and practical, especially if you don't have a heap of time!

Taking Charge of My Destiny

✓ Master the fear.

✓ Treat every lesson as an opportunity to be more of myself.

- ✓ Heal past blocks in my attitude or beliefs about myself.
- ✓ Heal old trauma and release its power over me.
- ✓ Draw a line in the sand.
- ✓ Choose a new perspective.
- ✓ Listen to my intuition.
- ✓ Be happy.

When I get to that moment where I've had enough of the pain, I love using this technique. It's like closing down the power of the past to hurt me. It's so simple and literally costs you nothing, and you can do it anywhere you are and anytime you're ready to leave the past behind.

Drawing a Line in the Sand

- Find an open space, ideally with soil or sand.
- Using a stick or your hand or your foot to draw a line in the sand about 2 m/6 ft long.
- Use your imagination if you don't have soil or sand available.
- Stand on one side of your line.
- Take 3 big breaths.
- Imagine the pain and the hurt of the past and allow yourself to feel it.
- Acknowledge the events of the past had a purpose: to get you to this moment.

- Give yourself permission to leave them in the past, where they belong.

- Imagine all the pain and hurt of the past, and let it go or put it down on the ground.

- Step over the line.

- Leave it there.

- Breathe and let go.

- It has no purpose or place in creating your today.

- Lift your chin and look forward.

- Take three big breaths.

- Invite the future to be bright.

- Walk forward into your future.

- Today is the first day of the rest of your life!

When you live this way, it awakens an awareness of what is real in your experiences. It becomes such an empowering way to live as you get to choose your responses rather than being pushed around by the actions or beliefs of others. Learning to identify what you think about reality does not make it your reality, rather it empowers you to choose how you experience it.

Think of how many thoughts move through your mind in an hour. They're not all real, nor are they all true. You let go of what isn't or doesn't serve you and you embrace what is/does. Experience is something temporary moving through your mind. It doesn't mean it's real and it doesn't have to be your truth.

Your experience can be changed.

You are in charge of your destiny with every choice you make.

You choose whether to see the world through fear and lack, or through love and an abundance of opportunity. Use the guided meditation in the next chapter to create a whole new way of looking at things.

Meditation: Perspective Shift

Do this meditation every week and at times of drama, fear or conflict.

Read or speak it slowly, with pauses at the end of sentences. Take yourself to a quiet space where you'll not be interrupted for a while. Turn off your phone, close the door and get yourself comfortable.

It's time to breathe, to let go.

We're going to help you to see the events of your life through a new perspective.

As you breathe, you are slowing each breath.

There's a sense of silence that is settling over you.

Each and every breath is making you more and more relaxed.

As you breathe you feel your breath passing past the confines of your lungs.

You feel as if you can breathe anywhere in the body.

Breathing slower and slower.

Your body knows now that it is safe.

Each and every breath makes you feel even safer.

As you breathe, you find your breath is naturally going into the heart.

Your heart responds and you can feel your internal intelligence and its wisdom being awakened as your body is dropping into peace.

Your body is beginning to really relax and is becoming heavier in your chair or where you're lying.

I want you to imagine using all your senses, seeing, hearing, feeling and knowing.

Imagine you can perceive what I'm describing.

Make it all up, if you need to.

Imagine for a moment that you are in a house.

Yet once you get inside, you find it has no windows, doors or exits of any kind.

How do you get out when you have nothing in the room to help you?

Your mind goes through a number of scenarios, but the room is solid, there is no getting out of here.

Then you remember to breathe into your fear, and there in front of you is your answer.

It's obvious.

Stop imagining!

Stop imagining and you won't be in the house any longer.

Imagine now that you are a person that you don't like or are not proud of.

How could you get out of being that person?

Could you become a new person?

Stop imagining!

The truth is that you already are that beautiful person you imagine.

Yet you have created a story around yourself, that you believe to be true.

That you are less or unworthy.

It's time to step out of that story, that life you find yourself stuck or unhappy in.

It's time to be really you.

But how?

I hear the question and I've lived the answers.

For me and for so many who seek me.

Who now likes who they are.

Come on a journey with me.

Imagine now, that you are in a ballroom, twirling, elegant men in suits and twirling women in beautiful ball gowns.

Your partner is an old sage, so full of wisdom and is guiding you into a new way.

As you twirl, you can feel and hear and see the opinions and the judgements of others.

You can see that some of these came from you ... assuming you knew what others were thinking.

Some are judgements that you've created of you.

All of them have attached at some time to your body.

As you twirl there's a magic happening and you notice that all of these judgements are levitating upwards from your body.

They're literally twirling away from you.

You're aware now that the ballroom has transformed into a room covered on every surface, with mother-of-pearl.

It's iridescence and brilliance is now permeating outwards and shining into you.

This brilliance is shining into you, meeting with your own inner brilliance.

You have become so expansive and can see everything with so much clarity.

Your spirit essence is showing you the brilliance that is you.

You feel such eternal joy and love and are limitless in the world.

Soon this joy and brilliance and love are seeping into your body.

You become aware of the room and its noises.

You feel the energy of the Earth centring you into your physicality and you have some water.

Slowly you return to your day, or snuggle into sleep.

Rewriting the Rules

As soon as the party was over, the stark reality of no distractions started to set in. All of a sudden, I'm a cancer survivor and I don't even really know what that means. I know I'm lucky to be alive, but the reality of having almost died is too confronting to contemplate. So, I don't.

I've been home from hospital for two months and I feel like nothing has really changed. Of course, everything *is* different. I feel fragile and unsettled as to my place on the planet. I know I've survived for a reason and what I have to do, yet I am so far away from feeling strong enough to do that.

In fact, that's what is missing—I don't have any strength.

You could say that cancer and the journey of its treatment and recovery have stolen away my strength, but the truth is that I lost it a long time ago. I've been weak for a long time and it's because I've been prioritising everyone and everything over what my body needs, and what *I* need to be happy.

My body has been trying to speak to me for a long time. I'm not really surprised I had cancer; there's been a lot out of order and I haven't been listening at all. I've put the needs of my body and soul last, and I've paid a very big price for that.

I feel at a loss really, there's just so much that needs to be changed and I'm not sure how to go about it. I don't even know all the answers as to why I had cancer in the first place. True, I know my body created cancer in response to me being sick in some way. I am not sick because I have cancer. My body has failed me.

Or has it? Perhaps the truth is that I've failed myself.

It is true. I have failed myself in so many ways and in so many decisions.

I know that I have to make changes, but where to begin? I make a list of what I can see as obviously 'lacking'. It doesn't take that long and it takes my breath away as I consider the enormity of just how many ways I've given myself away.

Lacking:

- Sleep
- Adequate water intake
- Healthful, home cooked meals
- Encouragement of me
- Passion
- Time to write and create new projects
- Creativity and art
- Time to enjoy my passions
- Time to learn and practice my guitar or a language
- Energy
- Exercise

Needing change:

- Fear
- Over-caring of my family, friends and clients
- Constant, over-critical judgement of my performance
- Hiding my brilliance

- Lack of time for stillness and meditation

- Lack of motivation to sustain change

- Over-patience with others

- Not enough date nights

In reading the list, it is abundantly clear that I am constantly prioritising myself last, leaving no energy at the end of each day for me. I'm living in an energy deficit every day, and it never seems to get better. In fact, it has become worse over time.

It is true I've been making significant changes towards improving these areas over the years and I'm way better than I was. Back then, the 'list of lack' would have been longer than a football ground. Still, despite the changes, I am still so over-committed. My inability to say no to everyone and everything has taken its toll. It's only since I've gone back to work that I'm starting to understand that normal people don't do what I do. It's impossible, the body just can't take it. It cannot sustain itself on occasional scraps of sleep, water, good food, stillness and exercise. It needs to be fuelled fully on a daily basis.

Where to begin?

My body got cancer. To get cancer, the immune system cannot have been able to recognise the tumour as something bad. It was either not functioning, or unable to function well enough to fight the cancer. All of these options speak of a body that has been pushed past its limits with very little, if any, in reserve.

I need to fuel my body, mind and soul to give it what it needs to be fully functioning and healthy. Some of that is physical, yet all of the mind, body and spirit aspects need to be full.

I like to tackle problems from the solution backwards to where I am standing. It just makes so much sense to break things down until the steps are small enough for me to manage. So, I look to how life *should* be, and I can see that everything has to change.

Some things are more important than others and some will be more difficult than others. Everything must undergo some sort of change.

I need to change the rules. All of them, as quickly as I can. Only then I can fuel my body. Who'd have thought it would be so huge? It's like I'm having a mid-life crisis.

I need to:

1. See myself as I am: brilliant, worthy and deserving.

2. Acknowledge that my needs are the most important of all. If I'm lacking, I cannot give.

3. Realise I deserve to be heard. No more staying quiet for the benefit of others.

4. Understand I need plentiful opportunities for sleep, rest, stillness and creativity, then ensure they happen.

5. Understand I need plentiful amounts of water, fresh food, exercise and passion, then ensure they happen.

6. Realise that being kind to me is always my first choice.

7. Ensure my environment is free of negativity: both people and places.

Wow! Is there anything that will stay the same?

Last Choice of Hero

When I was growing up, bad stuff happened to me. It was the sort of stuff a little girl should never have to face, let alone understand. I couldn't talk to anyone, and I assumed no one would understand. There was something different about me, something that people surely wouldn't want in their family or as their friend. I was a freak. I was broken and I was alone. I thought that I had been deserted by the place and souls I knew to be my spiritual home. I kept silent to be accepted.

I didn't know how to behave and I needed a hero to make me feel safe in the world. I looked to others for examples of how to behave. I copied those around me for almost everything. If I got in trouble, I looked for a hero to make the pain better. If Dad was the problem, Mum would be the hero, or Dad was the hero if Mum was the problem. If they were both the problem, Nanny or a teacher or Joan, my friend Fiona's mum, would be the hero. I looked outside of me for protection because the fear of what had happened was overwhelming.

I sought approval and love and attention from everyone. Parents, siblings, grandparents, teachers, friends, extended family and neighbours. I was starving for their stamp of approval on my worthiness. I was carrying some bad secrets and I had to constantly evaluate how I was being received. I couldn't risk them finding out the truth about me. I couldn't take the risk that Dad would find out and go shoot someone ... surely, he wouldn't shoot me? I'm being ridiculous! Then, as if on cue, he started talking about not having boyfriends. He said that if I brought a boy to the front door, he'd meet them with a shotgun.

Oh, no! What is happening now? Is he going to shoot them for kissing me? For being too beautiful? Because they love me like that? Of course, my common sense argued against this, I'd never seen Dad shoot or threaten a person with a gun. But he did shoot our dog when it was too sick to survive and was suffering, and he'd shoot rabbits for our dinner. When a friend was raped, he said he'd have shot the guy if it was his daughter. Didn't that mean it was possible?

I was so confused. I felt so much pressure to save the family. I didn't know who I was. I didn't know who I was supposed to be. I copied the behaviour of the other girls. I gained friends and I never really had any enemies. I got along with most everyone. But still I was hungry for love and having their approval was ever so important.

When a visitor once complimented my singing, Mum agreed, but she said that my sister was the talented singer in our house. Surely that meant I wasn't enough at that too. When I got a 'D' on my end of year report for typing, I was too scared to go home. I struck up the courage to tell her and she laughed. "Who cares about typing? I want to know you can read and write and do well in maths. That's what I care about."

At school if another student got a better mark on a test or assignment in those subjects, I'd be so disappointed and then terrified. I'd go home and tell my mother and she'd answer distractedly, as she juggled the four younger children and a mountain of housework. She didn't say much, most probably because I wasn't making her proud. Didn't my teacher always say that doing well at school would make our parents proud and happy?

No, I couldn't say she looked proud.

So, I'd hang out or fold the washing, or the peel potatoes sparingly to save as much as I could to make her proud. I'd distract and settle the children when she seemed sad or cross or busy. I became a little mother, hoping that it would make her happy. I took so much joy and love from her relief or her thanks. Surely this now meant that I was good enough, that I was making her proud? Would Dad be proud too? He was more interested in my brother and cars and football and archery and shooting and boy sort of stuff. He never seemed too interested in girl stuff. He was proud of football achievements, and girls couldn't play football.

My opinion of myself as I grew wasn't great. How can you think you're worthy when you believe yourself to be some sort of freak that needs to be hidden away? Would *you* rely on you, when you were something to be ashamed of? I could see people like me and they hid their gifts. Clearly, what we had was a bad thing. It must be. It was shunned by the community.

So how could it be safe to be me? If I hid my gift away, surely people would like me then. Surely if I copied how they behaved, I could be something great or, at the very least, maybe someone could like me.

We went to the races with my cousins one night while my mother had her weekly visit with my recently bereaved aunt. She was there to lend a listening ear and I was there to try to help the cousins forget their grief and have fun. I'm not sure how she thought I'd make it fun for them; we barely knew each other and I was younger, shy and unsure if they even liked me. They were friendly and had obviously been told to look after me.

The next week after I got home from school, my mother wanted a chat. That didn't sound good. What had I done now? Well, apparently, I was speaking with a plum in my mouth. I was too 'posh', according to my cousins' friends at the races. This was apparently not good, something else that was wrong with me. I'm sure Mum was hoping to help her shy, young daughter be accepted by other children.

I went around the corner to my best friend's Fiona's house. Joan, her mum, was like a second mum to me; she certainly treated me like her own child. She'd discipline us both, encourage us both to be the best we could be; to be highly educated, to get ahead in the world, and to present ourselves well. I loved it that she cared so much and I sought to please her whenever I could. There was none of the usual teenage daughter angst with me, and I was happy to chat with her forever.

I walked in the door and the tears started straight away. I reluctantly stammered through Joan's questioning about what had been said. She always helped me understand what was going on, but this time I saw a look on her face that I'd never seen before. She said she knew a lot about how to speak properly, and as long as I did what she told me, I would be welcomed through any door in town. She said those children were not yet educated or old enough to know what was right. I didn't know what 'posh' meant. She told me I was not to worry; she would take care of it. She was always correcting our speech, so I believed her. She always made me feel better, and as she hugged me, I thought she must be an angel.

I love her still for that. Her speech and elocution lessons have seen me walk into jobs without interviews and chosen for TV interviews. She was right. I can walk into any house in town and be well received. Not only did she reassure me, but as I was convinced of her intelligence, I took everything she said as a recipe for success. Funnily enough, it was.

Joan gave me self-confidence and showed me how to feed my belief in myself and to ignore the naysayers. She built on the words of my grade one teacher who supported my ambitious career choice, and expanded the love I received from my grandmother and some of the members of her family. I was so busy trying to keep out of trouble at home, and spent my time trying to please Mum so she'd never notice my lack again. I was so scared of disappointing her like the day after the sleepover. And as I grew into an adult and saw Dad with my children, I realised my interpretations were assumptions that didn't reflect his love for me. He was raising us along the typical lines of mothers raising daughters and fathers raising sons. It was the way of the time. I certainly didn't understand it back then.

If only I could have known then what cancer taught me. That instead of seeking others to love, feed and fulfil me, that I would be happier doing it for myself. That it would virtually wipe out disappointment, rejection, abandonment and self-criticism. If you are full, you don't need it from others, and therefore they'll never fail your expectations. Relationships would be happier, as you'd never be disappointed by their love not filling your need for it.

That if *I* was to choose *me* to be my number one hero, and not rely on someone else, I could be happy. I could be so fulfilled and happy with who I am.

I grew up looking for heroes, yet the best hero was looking right back at me in the mirror every single day. That hero would put me first, would have my back and protect me always. She would say 'yes' to love and 'no' to lack. She'd only allow great experiences and manage the lesser ones with alacrity and grace. She'd live intuitively and make life easy and happy every day.

I wish I'd known that it's easy when you choose to love you first. You always choose love and kindness for yourself. It feeds you, makes you feel whole, worthy, enough and ever so capable. The world just feels limitless. You're not exhausted from giving because you love yourself enough to say 'no'

When you are full, you can give fully to others. They are the icing on your already quite fabulous cake!

Action!
Becoming Your Own Hero

It's hard to be your own hero when you've spent years or even decades doing the opposite. I learnt the hard way that if I wanted to fill my needs for love and support, I needed to give it to myself rather than rely on anyone else to do it for me. What was interesting was that when I didn't need anyone to do it for me, extra love and support came from the most unexpected sources at the most unexpected times. It was like I had become a magnet for those wanting to support me by creating the vibration of self-care to attract it to me.

Supporting yourself is tricky when you have so many other demands on your time and attention. So, I came up with a recipe that would make it easier and help to keep me on track.

Becoming Your Own Hero

- Be your own best friend.

- Champion your causes.

- Learn to say 'no' when you mean 'no'.

- Say 'yes' to opportunities.

- Create from your mistakes.

- Make new friends.

- Find the things that make your heart sing.

- Look in the mirror and make you the hero.

Becoming your own Hero is easy, here's my recipe for each one individually.

Be your own best friend.

Most of the people who are reading this book are way better at being a friend than they are at self-caring. So, I think it's smart to use whatever strengths you've got when tackling a new or challenging problem. If you're a great best friend, start being your own best friend. Start caring for you in the way you do for others, spending the same amount of time fuelling your needs and desires and assisting you to have the best and easiest life. This one is a no-brainer. I promise you, you'll barely have to try.

Champion your causes.

You have no issue standing up and protecting those you love or care about, so use that same bravado and passion to stand up for you when you need it. If you agree with something, don't be afraid to show it and if you don't agree, be happy enough to show that too. What's the worst that can happen? People don't agree with you or judge you. That's great, we'd rather see the true colours of the people around us as it makes it easier to work out who to trust. If you find that the people around you are disagreeing more than agreeing, open yourself up to attracting in and finding a new tribe of people who'll better reflect and love who you are and what you stand for.

Learn to say 'no' when you mean 'no'.

So many of us say yes to people or things that we really don't like or want to do. We might be doing it to keep the peace or to please someone or to save their feelings. The problem is that doing this never makes you happy in the long run. Enough of this behaviour and you'll find yourself grumpy, impatient bitter and wondering when, if ever, it'll be your turn. Say 'no' when it honours you or empowers you to do so, don't make excuses or reasons and do it with confidence. Most people don't really care about the why's and will move on, e.g. "I'm so sorry Jessica, I can't come to your twenty-first birthday party tonight, but I don't want to miss out on celebrating with you. Could we do lunch or dinner or a drink next week?" And that's it, most people just want to know you care and this response makes that true.

Say 'yes' to opportunities.

Some of our greatest achievements came from opportunities or challenges that we were fearful about or felt significant resistance to. Use the fear mastery and live in the moment and then just do it anyway. I promise you it'll be way harder to live with regret than to deal with the outcomes of things not quite working out.

Create from your mistakes.

If things don't go well, look for what it is in the ingredients of what you're doing to find what is not in sync. When Richard Branson has a problem with one of his visionary ideas, he simply looks to what he can change easily to make the ingredients work together for success. Perhaps you needed more information, or maybe there is a better approach or there's someone whose advice you could seek.

Make new friends.

You cannot have too many friends. Friends are like seasons, they come and go, some seem to be around forever and others seem to disappear before you've had enough time with them. You never know who will bring joy to your life if you don't give them the chance to make it.

Find the things that make your heart sing.

Most of us have been too busy caring for everyone else that we've forgotten the things that make our heart sing. When our heart sings, we are in the happiest place of all, as we are feeding our spirit and feeling the joy that expands from that. Take some time out, perhaps over a cuppa or your favourite drink, and make a list of 25 things that make your heart sing. Look into your childhood, your teen and young adult years and magazines for ideas. If you can't finish the list, just work on it each day until you do. Then work on weaving those things into your life. It doesn't have to be every day, but ideally, you'd do at least one a week. When I did this, I reconnected to a passion for drawing and creating art.

Look in the mirror and make you the hero.

When you look in the mirror, resist the temptation to judge or criticise what you see. Instead, I'd like you to look for your strengths and congratulate yourself for all that you do well. Then look at what you perceive as your weakness. Handled well, every weakness becomes a strength, you just have to know how to use it. One of my weaknesses is that I'm hypersensitive to the pain or negative emotions of people. It could be said that I'm oversensitive and I could become the victim of that, or I could recognise that it's a great tool for being empathetic and supportive to people when they're struggling. Procrastination is another weakness that I've had over the years, but it does have its advantages. I never do something that doesn't feel right or that pushes me over what I can manage. My procrastination is actually like a set of brakes to my constant over-committal. When you look at yourself, give yourself a compliment or acknowledgment that is kind and supportive. Every time you look in the mirror, use it as a tool of encouragement. If you don't have a mirror, feel free to buy or borrow one and if that's impossible, do it all by imagining your reflection.

When you work at being your own hero, you guarantee yourself a life that is happier. Be patient with yourself and recognise that new habits can take forty days to become second nature, and old habits can take an agonising thirty days to break. If you fall back into your old habits, simply begin again. It becomes easier to honour you every time you try.

Meditation: What is True?

Do this meditation when you're having trouble seeing the brilliance that is you.

Read or speak it slowly, with pauses at the end of sentences. Take yourself to a quiet space where you'll not be interrupted for a while. Turn off your phone, close the door and get yourself comfortable.

It's time to breathe, to let go.

We're going to help you to see the truth that is you.

Your brilliance, your beauty.

As you breathe, you are slowing each breath.

There's a sense of silence that is settling over you.

Each and every breath is making you more and more relaxed.

As you breathe, you feel your breath passing past the confines of your lungs.

You feel as if you can breathe anywhere in the body.

Breathing slower and slower ... your body knows now that it is safe.

Each and every breath makes you feel even safer.

As you breathe, you find your breath is naturally going into the heart.

Your heart responds and you can feel your internal intelligence and its wisdom, being awakened as your body is dropping into peace.

You are becoming ever so relaxed.

So much so, that you imagine yourself to be in an old room.

The room feels old and comfortable and safe.

You are warm and it feels right here.

You see a full-length mirror in front of you with a very ornate frame.

You wander over to it, but find yourself standing to the side of the mirror.

You can admire it without seeing your own reflection.

The mirror is so beautiful.

It has been created by an artisan with great talent.

You feel drawn to stand in front of it, despite a resistance building inside of you.

This mirror is magical.

You can barely believe your eyes.

As you stare, you see the most beautiful soul, whose light is so bright, and so golden, and so beautiful, with a myriad of colours streaming through it.

This is the most incredible beauty you have ever seen.

You can see and feel so much love and warmth and gentleness and kindness and beauty in this soul.

You're astounded.

Who is it?

Who can it possibly be?

An angel.

A guide.

A special being of magic?

You're shaking your head in disbelief as the truth begins to dawn upon you.

That soul is very special, and is in fact the most special soul you've ever met, that you've ever known.

That soul is you!

You take some deep breaths.

The knowledge and the beauty of this soul have combined to take your breath away.

How can this be?

You think so much of yourself but none of it, not one bit of it, matches the truth of this soul.

This soul is beautiful and so very special; you can literally feel it.

How can this soul be you?

Your heart is spreading wide with every breath.

Each breath brings a great sense of love and healing through every cell of your body.

Old beliefs of your inadequacy and unworthiness are dropping away.

Space is being created for new ways of thinking about yourself.

You're feeling so beautiful and you can't really explain why.

It's your new truth, it's how people should be seeing you.

It's time to shine your light.

You can see the brilliance of the light of you.

It's brighter than halogen lights shining on a diamond.

It's time now, time to own it ... it's you.

You breathe in the brilliance that is you.

Your body is responding as it tingles throughout every part of you.

This is the brilliance that is you.

You'll shine it brightly from now on.

Each day, you'll learn ways to be safe being so brilliant.

There is nothing to fear.

You feel so happy, so full of love, as you become aware of the sounds of your environment.

Breathing deeply, you imagine your energy stretching down like anchors into the centre of the earth.

You drink some water, contemplating how different you feel and how different your world will become, one day at a time.

You rise slowly and return to your day or snuggle down to sleep.

You finally feel enough!

Struggling to Love Myself Again

So, I rewrote the rules and believed it would be a recipe for success. How wrong could I be? I was trying to rewrite almost five decades of behaviour in a day and that was a lot of change to create. I would never ask a client to create that much change so quickly. We work on one aspect, and when they've integrated the healing and created the changes that go with it, we move onto something else. My own personal plan and ideas on how to implement change in my recovery is a recipe for disaster.

I started with my body.

It's not going so well.

Despite a remarkable recovery, I have not had enough rest time. I needed a couple of extra months to replenish my depleted reserves. I am able to do the work, but I am still so tired, and I have to plan my activities. If it's a day to see clients, I do nothing else. We eat out so I can have a healthy meal with enough time to rest. I'm being mindful of just how much I'm doing. I celebrate being able to run a kilometre on and off, yet my mind yearns for my longer runs pre-surgery.

I'm super aware of the self-criticism thing, so I focus on encouragement and ignore the nagging voice of my ego, who seems intent upon destroying my every attempt at kindness. My body is still quite fragile, as my abdomen has had its length sliced through every layer. I'm seeing Kevin, my myotherapist, every week and he's insistent that I be careful about returning to exercise. I'm relieved, as I'm still so tired each day. I can clearly see how much energy my body didn't have before, as I take the time to listen.

My back hasn't been great since the surgery. I'm not sure what they've done in there, but within a couple of days in hospital, the pain was so severe that I needed a special mattress. With the hospital refusing to approve chiropractic care during my hospitalisation, my body got more and more unhappy. I had terrible pain most days. So, I'm working on it. Initially, I saw the chiropractor, but then I felt too fragile to continue. As soon as I could comfortably lie on my front, I returned to myotherapy. Those sessions have been wonderful. I've also chosen a new chiropractor closer to home and am having treatment. Mostly I'm feeling good, but I'm just not interested in exercising. I know it's important to me, but if I can't manage the energy, I'm not doing it.

Thankfully, my new choice of kindness to me is working, and I'm allowing myself the space to recover. I guess I'm not doing that badly, yet my soul is desperate for me to recover, so I can exercise again. I miss those happy hormones!

I'm working on the fresh food, but it's a challenge for me to work, run the family and cook a nightly meal. Truth is, it's been that way for a long time. Having problems with chronic anaemia meant I was often extremely tired as my levels dropped lower and lower. The combination of a pescetarian diet and heavy menstrual periods took their toll. I'm mostly eating healthy, and choose to eat at cafes and restaurants to ensure I'm getting what I need each day. If we have takeaway food, it's usually healthy. I gave up sugar when I was diagnosed, so on the whole, my food intake is okay. I'm just not cooking all of it.

Herein lies the trouble. I believe that a good mother and wife provides healthy home cooked meals for her family. So, every night when I haven't, I return to the old patterns of seeing myself as a failure. If I'm too tired to make love to my husband, I see myself as a failure as a wife, regardless of whether he's also too tired. If my children are critical of my efforts or how they see me, I spiral down into utter worthlessness. They have no idea what impact their criticisms are having. I've got enough acid in my own self-hatred to kill, I don't need any extra at this point coming from them. Initially they were pretty gentle, but they've no idea how fragile I am inside, how much everything hurts.

When I look at other mothers laughing and playing with their children, I am critical of myself for not being more fun. When I see children making their parents proud, I automatically look to where I might be failing. It's not even about my children or their behaviour. It's this continual need to thrash myself with my own meanness. When others annoy me, I berate myself for not being more tolerant.

My expectation of perfection and the cost to my self-esteem and self-worth has been staggering. If something wasn't perfect, if there was one little thing that could be perceived as being wrong, then I was a failure. Each instance proved it, and let's face it, if you're looking for proof of failure, it's pretty easy to find. I think of Leonardo da Vinci, who was one the most incredible artists and inventors ever. He held himself to a high account of perfection. His last words are said to have been, "I have offended God and mankind because my work didn't reach the quality it should have."

How could a man of his standing be critical in any way of the results of his achievements? Can we really not see our own brilliance?

Stop it! Stop it NOW!

It can and will be different, I just need to stop imagining that I'm terrible, not worth it, an imposter, a failure or—

My list could literally go on forever. It is time to stop it and give myself a break. Any kind of break will make a difference at this point. I am not so terrible. I am not a failure.

I look to what I do well and it's like anything I'm good at—I take for granted. I look to my work and know that others consider me to be a remarkable healer, many say that I've saved their life.

That, I can actually acknowledge. Over the years, it has been way too hard to argue with the constantly fabulous results my clients are able to achieve with my work. I'm making a difference and it's such a privilege to be a part of it. Over the years, I've achieved a reputation for my abilities as a healer, spiritual teacher and psychic.

Surely, I can manage these changes, I just need to take one thing at a time, allowing time to master each one. I do not have to build Rome in one day, and I have time to change what is no longer honouring my life.

I am taking it easy and supporting my body more. I'm meditating more, reading my books and playing my ukulele. Well, I'm trying to play the ukulele, Berni took my couple of lessons and mastered it in a minute. Okay, not a minute, but he did better than me. Wow! There I go again. Stop it now! You are not a failure because someone can do something better than you. It's time to get some healing.

It seems that for everything I do well or manage superbly, I have to find fault with something else. I'm starting to become aware of my patterns, and knowing where I'm heading empowers me to stop it. And I am stopping it.

I'm not failing at everything.

Some things I'm mastering and I'm learning a lot. I'm starting to see that I'm nowhere near as bad as I thought. Every time I love myself and am kind, I fuel more instances of love. I'm feeling more confident and more able to see a balance in what I can do, and what I'm learning to do.

It is just so empowering. I can't say that I'm finding it easy, but I'm using my old recipe for success, the one that pulled me out of depression.

Recipe to Master Change

1. What is really the matter?

2. Is it true?

3. Is it real?

4. What is the smallest thing I can change right now to make things better?

5. Each day I create one change if I can manage it.

6. If I don't feel I've mastered the change, or I'm not up to anything extra, I stick with yesterday's change and work on mastering that.

7. I give myself permission to fail and am kind when I do.

8. I ask for help whenever I can, and whenever I need it, I embrace it when it's offered to me.

It's making a difference. The above recipe gave me my life back as I ended my first marriage, when I was deeply depressed. I used it when I hit rock bottom and realised that no one was going to make this life better for me. I knew it was my responsibility to make every change, and along the way I needed to learn how to say 'yes' to help and 'no' to what failed to honour me.

I understand it now.

I hated myself sick.

I was too scared to be my full brilliance. My imagination and the stories I collected had told me I wasn't enough, but I know differently now. I know that I am a good person, that I have always been a good person! I know that I have hurt people along the way and for that I am so sorry. I have not hurt through malice, yet my inability to speak of how I felt, and the necessity to avoid conflict, meant that I haven't always done things right.

I'm learning and I've made mistakes. I might be making one right now, and that will be okay. I'll learn from it, and I'll be a better person for the experience of it. I'll be okay. Better to have learned than to never have taken the risk to fail. My greatest mistakes and the learning that comes from my greatest challenges are usually the things that have enabled me to evolve into who I am now.

I'm learning how to show myself to the world, to no longer hide. I'm learning to shine my brilliance and be okay with that.

Then, I was given my first opportunity to shine. My close friend Di, and her husband, Dave, had asked me to be a part of their wedding ceremony prior to my diagnosis, and today was their big day. I was wearing a beautiful silk dress, suede shoes to match and my hair and make-up were perfect. I was ready to stand up in front of so many people who knew my story and shine, despite them not knowing me well. I was alive and well and that is the best reason to celebrate.

I had written a personalised reading for their friend, and the most beautiful ring blessing ceremony. My job was to do the ring blessing with the congregation and to conduct their wedding vows as they exchanged rings. The celebrant then announced them as husband and wife. There was great joy all around and I felt so special. Although I was not authorised to marry anyone, they had created it in such a way that I felt like I had married them. Di was so excited later, telling me that was always their intention. I felt so blessed to have such a special place in their lives.

It was not hard to shine on such a special day, as we celebrated the enormous love of this beautiful couple.

Shining Your Brilliance

I f you loved yourself from the inside, you would see that nothing is or was ever wrong with you. Nothing lacking, not one thing. If you could only see what I can see inside you, you would fall in love with the brilliance that is you. If you could see what I can see, you would love yourself unconditionally and compassionately support and care for you in the seeking of your dreams. You would know there is no greater wisdom than that which speaks for the soul.

I know, I know, you're thinking we're a whole lot different, but that's only because you've got a negative voice in your head all the time, one that's mean, negative and puts you down while exaggerating your limits. I used to have that voice too, and boy was it insistent! When you are constantly being hassled by that voice, and let's face it, it's very loud, you can miss the voice of the soul.

The voice of the soul is beautiful, kind and so full of love and encouragement. The voice of the soul never puts you down when there's plenty of good to be acknowledged. And that's the difference, the soul can see the good in you, and the ego can only see the lack.

I was only ever dissatisfied with myself. It didn't matter what I did or was told, in my mind I was always inadequate. The criticism I'd taken over the years from nasty teenagers, selfish or unthinking people, and my ex-husband, took their toll. The sad thing is that being a healer just made me empathetic and compassionate to their side of things. How could I be angry at them if I understood their 'why' by looking into their eyes?

Yet I was angry. Rightfully or wrongfully, I don't know. It felt like I had been hurt a million times and I didn't think anyone loved me, except for my beautiful Nanny. She'd tell me how special I was, and that I was a gift from God, that I was here to do something special. She'd have dreams about it, and would say she was blessed to have me. She was a ray of sunshine in my day, phoning almost daily to have a chat about something or other. We got so much joy and comfort from each other. I was happier chatting to her than I was with my friends. Our connection held such love, that I never felt lonely when she was around.

She never questioned my decisions, until I told her I was moving in with my now ex-husband. She looked at me weirdly and asked me if I was sure. She was a very wise woman. I wish that I had been paying attention that day, or on the day before she died when she asked me if her pulse was okay. She was a medical miracle, having had the first pig heart valves inserted in Australia. She had lived an extra twenty-five years because of that. She had just been released from a hospital stay, where I was a trainee nurse. I had done everything to ensure that she had the best care, with full attention to everything, visiting her at least daily.

Two nights before she was discharged, I had a terrible dream. Sitting bolt upright in bed at 3 am, I was shaking, sweating and hyperventilating. I had just seen Nanny being worked on after a massive cardiac arrest, and I knew she wouldn't survive. Again, I tried to push away the reality of my situation, as that kind of dream has always come true.

She had looked at me weirdly that day and again asked me if I was sure about her pulse, so I happily complied and checked again. As I pressed on the artery in her wrist, her pulse was as strong and regular as it had ever been. I told her so, and she once again asked me if I was sure. I saw a glimpse of something she knew in her eyes, but was too scared to talk about it. She said she loved me and that she was proud of me.

That day she had been pulling all of her papers together, which unbeknownst to me, were sitting in a neat pile on her bedside table. When she unexpectedly sent me into her bedroom for her lipstick on the dresser, I didn't notice them.

She was dead the next day, well, technically, two days later. When my grandfather went for his nightly bath before settling, she lay down on the bed. I wonder, did she feel it? Was she scared? Oh, if only I'd listened, but I was so scared of losing her.

When Pa found her, he called my father, who called the ambulance. When my dad and my brother, Rick, arrived, the ambulance guys were giving her CPR. I asked Rick about it later. The picture, the clothes and the name of the paramedics were identical to the vision I'd had two weeks earlier.

They called me early in the morning and said that she was unconscious and in the hospital, but that it was best to go to work and they'd let me know. They declared her brain dead and turned off her life support just after my morning tea break. Despite racing back to the country to be with her, she died twenty minutes prior to my arrival. It was the exact same delay in getting approval from the matron to leave.

The world stopped turning for me that day. I was twenty and I did not know how to live without her. Being strong for everyone else numbed my painful heart, so I got stronger until the pain was buried. She was my world, I loved every part of her, the good and the occasional bad. I could not speak at her funeral. I was heartbroken. I knew I was to blame. I saw her death and didn't prevent it.

I should have saved her.

Every patient I nursed from that day benefited from her death. I nursed and cared and fussed over every patient as if they were her. All I could see was my failure and the need to do better and to anticipate every possible complication or emergency. I watched everything, avoided going on breaks if someone was very unwell or critical, and set up a pattern of over-giving. I had to make up for losing her. I would look around me to see if she was proud, but my ability to see the dead was gone. All I could feel was my grief and the enormity of my loss.

When I recovered, I over-cared for my fiancé. When my children were born, I took over-care to a whole new level. My children would never want for anything, and I did everything I could to prevent every possible negative incident. Over-protective probably describes me well. My intuition closed down after seeing Nanny's death, so I had to create control in my environment to feel safe. Being unable to control my visions created an indescribable terror. It meant I didn't want to look at anyone.

I didn't care about the personal cost to my mind, body or spirit. I had been trained as a nurse by religious nuns who advocated selflessness. I believed Nanny had died because of some lack of attention, or something wrong in me. So, I worked on becoming better.

When my daughter started seeing the spirit of Nanny at a little under two years old, I knew I had to recover my psychic ability. After my introduction to reiki and meditation, I went through a very rapid and powerful awakening. Soon, I could see and know almost anything. The more I knew, the further apart my husband and I became. I was severely depressed and unhappy all the time. Every day I'd act, put on my happy face and pretend to the world I was okay, that things weren't as bad as they seemed.

Because things were really bad.

Every day I woke up in tears because I'd survived the night. Every day I'd look at my husband as he made fun of me or criticised me at my most vulnerable times.

I wanted to die. I just wanted the pain to end, for his criticism to stop, for someone to truly love who would love me properly. Every day I would look at his judgment and feel like I'd failed, that my children would be better off with a mother who was perfect. Every day I was trying to be perfect and every day I failed.

Looking in the mirror I hated who I saw—someone who was a try-hard, someone who was a pretender.

My kids deserved someone who would set an example of a successful person to aspire to. I was a long way away from whoever that woman was. I wanted stillness away from the noise of his voice and from my inner voice, as both of them felt like they were already killing me.

I wanted to go back to my spirit home where I knew I was wanted and loved.

But I had one big problem. Two very precious children who I loved more than anything or anyone on the planet. I could not leave them alone with their father to raise them, so I chose to live.

So many nights I'd lay in bed, long after he fell asleep, wondering if I was the problem. Surely, I couldn't be as bad as I thought. His harsh words as we argued seemed valid and gave me a new taste for a bigger healing.

After my first Sekhem healing with Ida, painful sex disappeared. The birth trauma I'd experienced was gone, and with those blocks gone, I now had the chance to rebuild my relationship with him. So, I tried. I tried really hard.

Every argument, he'd criticise or verbally attack me, and at every healing, I'd heal that and anything else I thought could make me better. Surely if I healed everything that made our misery my fault, he'd be happy and I'd earn his love. Every criticism gave me the motivation to be better and with each healing, I was getting happier. I was no longer lacking in hope; I had friends on a spiritual path and I'd reconnected to my psychic ability. Life was looking good, unfortunately, just not in my marriage.

And all of a sudden, I could clearly see my mistake.

I had married a man who was mostly good, but he was not the right recipe for me.

It was like I was a 'round' peg in his 'square' hole. I couldn't fill the requirements of what he wanted from a wife, and with each passing day I wanted out of the marriage more and more. We were turning each other into terrible versions of who we were when we met. The amount of fighting between us showed he didn't like who I'd turned into, and I certainly didn't like who he'd become.

When I left the marriage, I became the topic of gossip between people I didn't even know. I was to blame and I couldn't argue with that. Yet the outcome of our marriage was not my fault.

We both killed our marriage.

It didn't matter, and so I walked away. I refused to gossip or tell people why I left. I had my own reasons and they were private. I didn't want the children exposed to gossip and I knew my now ex-husband would cope better if people didn't know about it. I needed them to support him, so that he would recover from our divorce well enough to care properly for our children. It was no one's business and the welfare of my children was paramount.

As soon as I left the marriage, it was like I had been set free. I began to see the world differently. I was alone, but never lonely. My heart was singing with joy, although it ached when my kids missed their dad, or me when they stayed with him. I gave them healing every night as they fell asleep, and was so grateful that I'd followed my intuition to learn to heal. I wanted them to be happy and they were loving having this happy mum.

In retrospect, it's pretty clear that something was missing for me to be so unhappy.

What I was missing was me.

Each time I worked on myself, I began to see that I was a great person and that people actually liked me. The friends that chose to support me on my journey were incredible supports. Fran, Monica, Tracey, Paul and Bernard held my hand through everything. Their ability to love me for me is something that I hold very dear—without it I couldn't have shone so brightly.

The happier I became, the more I let down my guard. I was dancing to music with the kids all the time, singing in the car and in the supermarket. I was spontaneous and loving and free. I had fabulous friends. People were remarking about my glow, the sparkle in my eyes and my infectious smile. Not every day was fabulous, but I'd not had this much happiness in years. We went out, socialised heaps and I felt very safe in my little house.

Change was afoot.

Maddie, Lachy and I went over to Bernard's house for a barbeque with his kids. I was so grateful for his support through my divorce, and even his very misguided advice for the last year of my marriage to 'keep trying', 'find a spark', and 'give everything a go'. He had no idea what I was living, but he'd been through the hell of divorce himself, and was just trying to prevent me experiencing the same pain.

I went to give him my standard hug and kiss on the cheek, and found him kissing my lips instead. I'm not sure who was more shocked. I was not far out of my marriage.

I think I loved Bernard from the day I met him, but had no idea what real love was, because I never had it in my marriage. We were friends, good friends, and I was unwilling to risk that friendship.

It didn't stop five-year-old Lachy singing at the top of his voice, "Mum and Bernard sitting in a tree, K-I-S-S-I-N-G!"

We circled around each other for a while, neither of us sure if I was ready. All I knew was that I was happy, and the happier I was, the more happiness I attracted.

My guides were telling me to love him.

My mind was screaming it was too soon.

My heart won.

I think he must have had my heart from the beginning.

Action!
Abundance: Your New Reality

The brighter I shone, the happier I was. The happier I was, the more abundance followed me. The greater I opened my heart through healing and allowing myself to be loved, the greater the abundance became. It was like our joy was directly connected to the state of our bank accounts. When Berni and I moved in together, it was a catalyst for so much love. This massive expansion of our ability to love and be loved was matched with the expansion of our wealth, happiness, and joy. It just never seemed to stop.

I had struggled financially as a single mum for a long time, as all our savings were invested in our mortgage, and it took almost a year to sell the house. Living week to week was tricky, but as usual, I had this deep faith that we would always have what we needed. This theory was tested multiple times as the bills mounted over my meagre income. I could barely work unless the children were with their father, as I could no longer afford childcare. I wanted to ensure they were loved through the transition and did the best I could.

We ate every night so that was good!

The secret to abundance is your heart. If your heart is open and you are happy, you'll attract ample abundance into all of the areas of your life. I created a workshop and a CD of guided healing meditations called *Living and Embracing Your Abundance*, as it became clear I had a knack for pulling abundance toward us.

If you look after yourself and your energy, your bank account directly reflects that. When you start loving yourself and living that way every day, you become a magnet for 'gold' (a plethora of everything you yearn for and desire). When you understand, there's a great motivation for ensuring a positive energy and matching emotional state. You feel motivated to let go of old pain, to leave the past in the past, and to create more and more joy. Life just keeps getting easier.

But how to do it? My recipe for abundance looks like this.

Abundance Recipe

1. Breathe and find stillness every day.

2. Forgive well and often.

3. Leave the past where it belongs, in your history.

4. Open your heart and risk being loved.

5. Love and kiss with abandon.

6. Dance to the music of life as often as you can.

7. Imagine that which you desire, by focusing on the feelings of being there.

8. Spend a lot of time daydreaming about the desire.

9. Ignore the lack, regardless of how hard it is, do not give it your attention.

10. Breathe in abundance every time you face lack.

11. Live and breathe the gratitude for all that you have, even the little things.

12. Bless the bills and know they'll be paid.

13. Seek joy in everything.

14. Seek joy every day.

15. Be joy!

You don't need anything else. It speaks for itself when you are living by loving yourself, even if you are just starting the process.

Just be kind to yourself, breathe, and be patient and focus on what you want, rather than what you lack. It's not about being greedy. It's about loving yourself enough to create ease and grace in your life. Comfort comes along with that.

Let's get loving you and getting positive!

Journey Back to Me!

It's my birthday! I've actually made it! I burst into a flood of tears. I thought this day might never come.

My tumour was diagnosed as very aggressive, and according to the medical world, you're lucky to survive this type of cancer. It feels like a miracle, but I know how much healing and medical work has gone into it. I'm so grateful for having found it when I did.

I wake early and spend the quiet time before the household wakes in gratitude, reflecting on what has been one hell of a year. Who would have thought on my birthday last year, that I would travel such a path?

I think of all the support I've had over the months since my diagnosis. It has been five months now. I think of last week when I had my first follow up scan and check-up. A week before, I began to get nervous and had to work hard on mastering my fear. Having the scan brought back all of the trauma of my hospitalisation with a thud. It was like being hit by a truck. The radiation from the scans also hit me like a truck. But Berni was there, smiling his big dopey smile at me. How can I worry with this man walking beside me?

The day before my appointment with the doctor, I meditated deeply and returned to my natural state of knowing and faith in my destiny. I know that I do not die from this, I know I can't see any cancer in my body again. I relax. The results are already in. I can't, nor do I need to change anything. What I can already see is a clear set of scans.

I think of how wonderful I felt when I walked in to his office. He was delighted to tell me that of course I was right, my scans are clear. Okay, he didn't actually say I was right, ha-ha. I am now allowed to extend the frequency of my scans and check-ups to every four months instead of three.

He was surprised by my attitude and just how positive I was being. I told him that I plan to never, ever have a conversation with him about there being cancer in my body again. I'm choosing to use these appointments as an opportunity to celebrate the success of my treatment. He's happy to go with that, although both his doubt and his hope that it could be true are obvious beneath his smile.

We celebrated later at one of our favourite restaurants, such a brilliant night of memories.

We were all so happy!

I am woken from my memories by a very excited little boy who can't wait for me to open his best birthday presents ever! I shake myself back to the present, as I smile at his joy. Zavier and I share a super excitement for the joy of special occasions, and Berni loves making them special. At his request, I've given him a long list of present ideas to cover my birthday and Christmas presents. As my family join me throughout the day, it appears that he's gone overboard. I have everything on the list, and Christmas is still a month away. I am one lucky girl!

Dinner is fabulous with the family. I just love our kids, and gathering together to share a meal brings me so much happiness. It's the most perfect birthday. Berni makes a toast to long life, health and happiness. It seems so surreal to be here, I just can't stop drinking in the moments, filling myself with the most marvellous memories.

Two days later, I'm on a plane to Bali with my sister to celebrate her fortieth birthday and my beating cancer. We find ourselves in the beautiful Viceroy Bali resort in Ubud, which is perched on the top of a valley with views to the Mount Batur volcano. The energy here is incredible and I'm so emotional. This trip had been planned prior to cancer and it's so weird to be here without the safety net that Berni has provided me over the last months.

The tiredness hits me hard that night. I normally travel so well, but I think the torrent of emotional upheaval over the past few months has taken its toll. I'm asleep just as my head hits the pillow. I seem to have lost the ability to stay awake past what my body can tolerate.

I love the energy of this place and the resort is so beautiful, with such amazing food that we barely leave it to go sightseeing. The staff all know who we are and what we're celebrating and they're going out of their way to make this a memorable stay for us both. Sitting next to the infinity pool reading is wonderful— finally time to myself that isn't coloured by cancer. I need a rest and this is the perfect antidote; it literally feels like we're sleeping on a huge crystal. Swimming in the pool is so refreshing, and the energy of the water and the place feels like it's actually healing me. I know this is why I've come to Bali, to soak in this place.

My body was healing, but now my spirit, which has been so battered, is soaking up a healing balm.

Taking time out is showing me just how much I have given to others over the years. I've willingly given out thousands of hours and dollars to assist others with their day to day problems. Healing or helping them all just seemed part of what I was there to do.

I set myself free from the promises I had made to myself and to Nanny to look after everyone.

It is my turn to look after me.

In the clarity that comes from meditating so much, I see that my body couldn't have fought the cancer. It had nothing left after giving everything away. I use the trip to focus upon feeding my mind, body and spirit.

Christmas has always been a very special time for me, less because of the religious significance and more because the anniversary of Nanny's death falls a week prior. That first Christmas was hard, but I was determined to bring the joy that Nanny would have on the day. My heart was hurting and we were all grieving.

I thought of her asking me to look after them all for her, as I took her pulse that last time. Christmas had been her thing, one of the few times she could celebrate her deeply religious beliefs with her family. My parents decided long ago that their children wouldn't receive any religious education. She was devastated and would pray for us all each day. She managed to sneak in the Lord's Prayer, but that was about it.

When I celebrate Christmas, I see her face and her excitement and it matches my own. It's the only time I get to give lots of gifts to everyone I love on the same day. I love the gathering together and this year we're keeping it very intimate. Elyse and Dylan's mum, step-father and half-sister, and my friend, Alesa, join us. I've created special surprises in the bonbons, and I'm so excited for the day. Alesa's family is in Sydney, so it's nice that she's sharing her special day with us.

I also love that we can share special occasions with Berni's ex-wife and her family. It's so beautiful for the four of us and for our kids—they don't have to worry about trying to stretch their day to cover all of us. People find it strange that we're choosing to spend Christmas together, but I'm proud that Berni and Lauren have worked hard on creating harmony and healing their issues with each other. I wish Maddie and Lachy could have that too.

I'm emotional in the morning, but I have no time to linger on that. Berni has turned on the built-in barbeque to cook the pork using its oven function. As he turns to ask me how many pancakes I'd like for breakfast, his face goes white as he swears loudly. I can't imagine why he's swearing, but as I turn I see flames coming out of the barbeque and up the wall to the ceiling of the pergola. The whole area is black with smoke!

Grateful for my years of emergencies as a nurse, I act quick, grab the fire extinguisher I bought for just this purpose, and the fire is extinguished. There's black smoke and smudge everywhere—thankfully, I hadn't decorated and set the table yet!

It takes ages to take the heat out of the fire as it sits in a stone bench and is backed by a marble wall. That and our quick actions with the availability of the fire extinguisher no doubt saved the house.

I'm so happy and shout it out on Facebook, with photos showing the damage. Berni is bemused, and I'm emotional at lunch. I don't think our kids really understand the enormity of what we've been through; the outcome of protecting them from the worst of the worry and trauma. I feel so grateful; I'm alive and living in a house that has not burned down.

How does it get any better than that!

Meditation: Becoming Kind

Do this meditation as an antidote to being critical as often as you like.

Read or speak it slowly, with pauses at the end of sentences. Take yourself to a quiet space where you'll not be interrupted for a while. Turn off your phone, close the door and get yourself comfortable.

It's time to breathe, to let go.

We're going to help you to find kindness within, to become kindness to all that is you.

As you breathe, you are slowing each breath.

There's a sense of silence that is settling over you.

Each and every breath is making you more and more relaxed.

As you breathe you feel your breath passing past the confines of your lungs.

You feel as if you can breathe anywhere in the body.

Breathing slower and slower ... your body knows now that it is safe.

Each and every breath makes you feel even safer.

As you breathe, you find your breath is naturally going into the heart.

Your heart responds and you can feel your internal intelligence and its wisdom being awakened, as your body is dropping into peace.

Your body is beginning to really relax and is becoming heavier in your chair or where you're lying.

As you feel your awareness beginning to float out of your body, you are super aware of all of your senses.

What you're feeling, seeing, hearing, and what you know.

You find yourself to be in a large room, in what looks to be a silver palace.

You're using your imagination, and all of your senses to create this experience.

It's just happening without you trying, you don't have to see.

In this palace, there is a great feast set at a very long table.

But as you look closer, you are surprised to find that the table is not filled with food.

Each person appears to have a place set for them, their name appears on a card naming the event.

The table of kindness.

You're fascinated and drawn to the chair with your name in a daze, there is so much to take in here.

Grandly dressed waiters appear out of nowhere with fresh water.

They indicate for you to take from the bowl in front of you.

As you do, you are surprised to see the bowl is filled with the most delicious looking sweets.

They feel like love.

You reluctantly take just one, and realise it is not edible and is instead an alive looking ball of colour.

You intuitively place it on the tip of your tongue and as it explodes, find that your taste for life has been altered into a state of receiving love.

This all feels like a scene from *Alice in Wonderland*, but you are too fascinated to care.

The waiter indicates another dish and you find there is a pink peg.

As you pick it up, it automatically clips onto your nose.

You are now smelling roses.

As soon as it is there, it is gone.

You're getting the hang of this and you're eager to have more.

You pick from the next bowl and find it's a small jar of oil which you intuitively place in various parts of your body.

Criticism is deleted away.

You can feel the joy lifting within you.

What else is there?

You pick from plate to plate, each time finding a little bit of joy as the items dissolve away your old patterns of being harsh with yourself.

And then you feel like you're done.

You feel full.

You feel happy.

All of a sudden, your failures look like learnings and you feel indulgent as to just how far you've come, just how much you've learnt.

Your tongue has changed and your mind has altered its patterns to match.

You are wired for kindness, although you can't find the item that actually made that happen.

Old ways of being harsh or critical will no longer feel comfortable, and you'll find yourself seeking ways to be kind.

You feel new criteria building within your mind.

Acceptance is a state of allowing yourself to be you, in all of who you are in the moment.

Perfection.

You feel comfortable with your current state of perfection, knowing you are happy with who you are.

You're perfect being you.

Protection.

Is building within you, not as barriers but rather as a strength to withstand the negativity and judgements of others.

Willingness.

To learn is flooding through you like a blanket of the most brilliant gold.

Expanding.

The kindness that you give to others.

You feel that kindness now extending and expanding into you.

Generously.

Is how you're now seeing your learning efforts during your walk through this life.

Your heart is opening.

You feel forgiveness for you flooding through your heart.

All you can see is the most iridescent magenta coloured pink.

You feel the love and the passion that comes with this energy permeating throughout every cell in your body.

You feel enough and now also feel brave enough to fail or succeed trying.

Life feels very safe regardless of the challenges ahead.

Your eyes are changing to be able to see the silver lining in each situation.

You become aware of the room and its noises and gently open your eyes, stretching back into your body.

You drink some water and then rise into a new you.

Life begins today with a new attitude and a willingness to be kind.

As you walk into your day or snuggle into sleep, you do it with a smile. Nothing will ever be so bad again!

Action!
Recognising the Self-Hate

You might be wondering why we need to action self-hate here. Haven't we just learnt how to be kind? I find it is more efficient this way, because in my experience we are unable to really look at self-hate with any clarity if we haven't first learnt the behaviours of kindness. Doing things in this order prevents you from spiralling down into further criticism and self-hate. I found that the more kindness and acceptance I had for myself, the more emotionally capable I was to acknowledge how I had been judging my performance in life.

Everyone suffers in some way from self-hate, although they may not see it as such. Most of us think of or remember our past experiences for the emotion, rather than the results. Self-hate is actually the energy that gets stuck as a result of an experience of inadequacy. That energy can get shut in anytime we experience one of eight emotions.

Self-hate is the trickiest energy that we find stuck in the body, and the hardest to heal to its core. When we work with Meliae Intuitive Healing, that's what we're doing—looking to heal the causative core. So many people live with hate because it has snuck up on them and are quite unaware that it's there. When you look into the body, it looks like poison!

The problem with healing hate is that it's like a chameleon. Hate is the master of disguises. It lives energetically in the liver, the sinuses, the gall bladder, the intestines and the joints. It will store as bitterness or anger, each creating an acidic effect in the energy of the body. The body reacts to insulating itself from the effects by surrounding the anger with fat, or if it is unable to do so, buries it in the folds of the intestines. The fat comes and goes, and can become particularly stubborn in later years. If it sits in the intestines, it will create an inflammation or dysfunction that prevents nutrient absorption or creates nasty side effects, like bloating and pain.

So how do you find it and how do you get rid of it?

The great thing about hate is that you can literally stop it in its tracks by recognising its behaviours and interrupting its patterns. You can stop your body deteriorating further by responding to the hate right now. Once you can recognise where and how it turns up for you, you have space to start embracing love and joy. You can start connecting to others in a profound and loving way. Those you want close, who deserve to be close, will be embraced in such love. Those who you choose to distance yourself from will hardly know you're alive and you'll be happier without their negative effects. I'm not suggesting everyone will disappear, but you'll be less affected, or possibly not at all.

Hate is tricky, but you can be trickier, so I've made it easy for you. Keep in mind that this chapter is about dealing with the hate *now*. Healing old and supressed hate takes some time and is complicated by our inability to let go of more than a bit at a time.

The problem with hate is that it builds up, and becomes part of how we define ourselves. Bit by bit, as you change your behaviour, so too will the hold hate has over you. Bit by bit, it will start to let go and leave you alone. The hardness that has built up will drop away.

What I find fascinating about hate is the way how it slowly builds in the body. You don't recognise it because it's just a little bit at a time. The other reason we don't see it is because we avoid the *story* of the emotion; it makes you feel uncomfortable.

Each emotion that becomes stored as self-hate, does so because of your unwillingness to feel or face your perceived inadequacy. You don't store anger because your brother stole your toy, you store it because you were disciplined for not sharing. Maybe you were sharing and it didn't look like it, or maybe you just needed a moment with your special toy. But after choosing to feed your own needs for a minute, you're made to feel damn guilty about it!

So, each of the emotions has a common theme that suggests or implies your inadequacy in some way. You didn't store jealousy because your sister got a new doll or a special cuddle. You stored it because she got the praise about being so 'good' at a time that you were not 'good'. It's like her treatment is rubbing salt into your wounds and they're making such a deal of how 'good' she is, and by default, how 'bad' you are. It hurts more than they know.

Let's look at the disguises of self-hate.

- Frustration

- Jealousy

- Anger

- Anxiety

- Bullying

- Control

- Deception

- Loneliness

I imagine you weren't thinking of this cocktail of emotions when I was talking about self-hate. We experience all of them in varying degrees and don't always deal with them well. That's the point really, we all have them at some time—none of us is exempt. It's the *degree* of our emotional pain that manages to infiltrate our thinking and being. As we are feeling it as the emotion, we assume it's just the emotion. But what's happening is that pain of inadequacy *behind* the emotion, those feelings of being 'bad' or unworthy, are being stored within your body. It won't be remembered, as it slips unseen through our filters and into the sub-conscious.

What's really tricky is that our feelings of inadequacy are small in comparison to our pain, and so are usually invisible to our attention. It's like the conscious brain acts like a colander, holding the big things in its memory, but allowing the little invisible things to slip through. So, that's where the inadequacy goes, and if there's enough, it will start to affect the psyche or the physical body in a really bad way.

When something sinks into the subconscious, you have no awareness that it's there. That's why we've had such success with Meliae Intuitive Healing, which does its best work on the subconscious. The healer has the ability to listen to the subconscious and work with the soul energy of the body, which has the capacity to heal. It's the pathway of finding that which is preventing you from living a full and free life.

We're all intelligent enough to know that if something hurts, you remove whatever is causing the hurt. If we burn our finger on fire, we move the finger away from the flame.

The problem with self-hate is that you can't see it to remove it.

It's buried there for a reason—to avoid experiencing the hurt. It sits in the subconscious if it cannot be processed or healed at the time by the psyche. If you have an incident and work through the emotions and the hurt, it doesn't stick. Perhaps you're too young or don't have the time, willingness or even maturity to process it. It's this reluctance to face the stories and the pain around the hurt that gets it stuck.

If you can process an incident within the first week or two by chatting to a trusted person or thinking it through, it disappears. Unfortunately, if we avoid it or don't process it, the energy will get stuck. What's great is that no matter when it happened, it can be healed and life can return to normal. You just need to know how.

The great thing about the guided meditations in this book is that they feel very familiar, which makes it quicker to drop into the healing space. They're designed to allow you to process and heal what has become stuck.

If we knew that our body held the residual, or even all of the negative energy of our amplified emotions within our body, we'd be a whole lot more conscious about how we deal with our day to day life. If we knew that we could avoid long term damage to our body and our psyche by managing these incidents at the time, would we react and think differently?

Maybe. Maybe not.

If you're ready to do it differently, let's look at how we can take hate's power over you away and throw it away forever!

Frustration

Frustration is the one behaviour that we most easily relate to. It's a harsh energy and it doesn't need a lot to make a negative impact. It removes you from your place of centre and comes as a result of measuring yourself against an immeasurable or unreachable ideal. This ideal will have become set before you were seven years old, and as such has long been forgotten. When you can't see just where you've set the bar for your behaviour, you start to look to others for examples of how to be good.

Frustration is a problem for self-hate when:

- you just can't do it, and are pitied for your results

- you can't find the words to express yourself

- you hurt someone and are singled out for your behaviour

- your intelligence is not recognised and you're made to feel stupid

- you are misunderstood and thought to be stupid in some way as a result

- you feel like you could have done better, particularly if you gave less than 100% effort

- you're ridiculed or teased for your performance and your vulnerabilities

- things take longer than anticipated, and you are letting others down as a result

- you perceive you're being treated inequitably because you're not good enough

- you're under pressure to perform and feel like you are failing

- you're late and someone suffers negatively as a result

- the outcome isn't what you'd anticipated, and people knew it mattered to you

- people aren't doing it your way, and are less efficient or successful as a result

- people aren't listening, or you get interrupted when speaking

- you don't receive what you'd been hoping for and see it as a betrayal

- people are mean to you when you're too tired or upset to know it's not true

- you watch others being mistreated and feel helpless to intervene for them

- you feel helpless to create change or the outcomes you desire due to your sense of inadequacy

Remedy for Frustration

Ask yourself if it's true that you're inadequate in this situation. Or is it that you are learning a new skill or seeking new knowledge? If so, let it go! Each of us deserves a chance to learn!

Ask yourself if your 'lacking' is something you should already know, have or do. If so, what is blocking you using the information or action? Choose to bypass the block consciously, by mastering your fear and doing it anyway.

Ask yourself if the pressure you or others have put upon you, is getting in the way of you achieving your best. If so, stop it or try to limit your exposure. Seek to prioritise moments where you stop, breathe and re-centre. Meditate as often as you can.

Ask yourself if not being seen is really the problem. Why do you need the attention of that person? Can you fill that need yourself, so you can be more neutral rather than needy in your interactions? If so do it now, if not, get help to learn how to do it now.

Ask yourself what is the smallest thing you could do right now to change this situation. Then go ahead and do it. This is a good habit to create in each of your activities of every day.

Jealousy

Jealousy is an insidious energy and can become so ingrained that it doesn't appear to be something that you need to notice. Jealousy is when you step outside of your own brilliance, unable to see just how wonderful you are. When this happens, you are looking to others and seeing your inadequacy, rather than seeing them as potential inspiration to see your own worth once more.

Jealousy is a problem for self-hate when:

- people have something you want and you hate them for it

- you feel different and are too shy or scared to be yourself
  you look different to others and are humiliated for it

- you have less freedom than others, and wonder 'why can't I', and thus make yourself a victim

- you get less love from others, and feel it's because they're better than you

- you get less attention than others, and feel it's because they're better than you

- you're just not special, and someone else is getting the love *you* deserve

- you're not being heard, and your opinion doesn't matter

- you can't afford it, and you feel like this makes you a loser

- you miss out on being included, which proves how you're not wanted and therefore unacceptable to everyone

- you have less power than others, and feel 'lacking' or inadequate

- you have little or no choice compared to those around you, and therefore feel like you're not important to others

Remedy for Jealousy

Ask yourself when, at the times you feel someone is being favoured over you, if that is true. If so, is that person doing this to help you be a better person or to facilitate better behaviour? If so, let it go. It has no bearing over you as a person.

Ask yourself if someone is actually better than you. Different is not always better. Popular is not always happier. Prettier is not always more loved. What we believe to be important and the people who we think get it, are not necessarily the ones who achieve the success, popularity or fame when they're older.

Ask yourself if you are actually liked or not. Is it because you're feeling out of sorts or sensitive at the moment? If it is true, is it because this person or people are not your tribe? Your tribe are the people you spend time with, who see and feel the world like you do. It's okay to be different to other groups, you just need to find the group who match who you are.

Anger

Anger is the explosion of negative energy that occurs when our spirit is not being heard. It may stem from any of the other emotions we are focusing upon, but it has a lower vibration and higher intensity to your awareness. This is your soul's way of getting your attention, resetting your pathway into actions, beliefs and behaviours that honour you. It's just that sometimes we get caught up in the emotion and miss the message.

That only serves to amplify the anger. It lives on the inside and is like a volcano. As soon as you can't handle how much you're carrying, there'll be an explosion to vent this very negative energy. The problem with anger in self-hate is that the emotion gets all caught up in the anger of the experience. You're so busy being angry, that you don't even notice the inadequacy inside the anger slipping through.

Anger is a problem for self-hate when:

- you know it's not right and you're still doing it

- you fail when you know you didn't try at all or to your full capacity

- you feel inadequate when you compare yourself to others

- you could have done better, and you berate yourself for not knowing how

- you're too scared to do things, and therefore miss out on everyone else's fun

- you're betrayed by someone you trusted or believed in

- you're abandoned by someone you trusted or believed in

- you're left out by someone you believed you should have mattered to

Remedy for Anger

Ask yourself why you're doing what you're doing. If you know it's wrong, stop it now, or make the choices/take the actions to get you away from the behaviour or situation. Follow your intuition.

Ask yourself if it is true that you're actually inadequate in this situation or just scared. Or are you are learning a new skill or seeking new knowledge? If so, let it go! Each of us deserves a chance to learn! If you're scared, master the fear and do it anyway.

Ask yourself if that person who has let you down was someone you should have trusted, or did you intuitively know better? If so, choose better people, open yourself to new relationships or friendships. Don't assume bad choices you've made about people in the past will continue. Breathe, become still, and trust your intuition.

Anxiety

Anxiety is a symptom of your personality being disconnected from your soul wisdom. Your intuition and its internal radar are unable to perceive where there is risk, and where there is none. Your anxiety stems from the combination of this intuitive block and a feeling you are in impending danger. Most anxiety is unfounded. We spend a greater percentage of our life worrying about things that never happen.

Anxiety is a problem for self-hate when:

- something is unknown, and you don't feel equipped to face or do it

- you've watched others fail at what you're trying to achieve, and thus you expect you will too as you're less than them

- people more qualified appear unsuccessful or inadequate, so what hope is there for you?

- you've failed at something before, thus you must be some sort of a loser

- you've had a hurtful or upsetting experience in this situation previously, so you feel inadequate in preventing the hurt from happening again

- you feel you're alone or unsupported because of some perceived inadequacy

Remedy for Anxiety

Master your fear! None of this stuff exists or matters if you master your old patterns of fear. None of this will hang around once you have mastered the fear in the situation. Use the fear mastery you learned earlier in the book to create instant results.

Bullying

When you are disconnected from your spirit and unable to see the true worth of who you are, your fear takes hold and starts to behave badly. Bullies mistakenly believe that if they behave this way, no one will have the time or opportunity to see what it is that's lacking in them. If you are being bullied, your inadequacies likely mirror their own.

Bullying is a problem for self-hate when:

- they go for your vulnerabilities which only adds to your feelings of inadequacy

- their behaviour proves just how pathetic you are

- you can't protect others because you can't protect yourself, which makes you feel even more pathetic

Remedy for Bullying

Do the 'Daily Reset to Spirit' guided meditation from chapter three daily.

Ask yourself if those who are behaving like bullies are doing so because you're inadequate, or because they fear you seeing the inadequacy in themselves.

When we feel out of control or at risk, we'll behave in a way to protect that risk. Once you see their inadequacy, it will mean you'll react differently. If the way you react changes, so does their ability to find your weak spots, and thus take away or have power over you.

Ask yourself if it's your job to protect others. Most times we have created these patterns of behaviour when we were young children. At that time, you were probably too young or as a child it was not your job to protect, it was your job to be protected. This is a habit that can be broken—you are not that young child anymore.

Control

When we are disconnected to our spirit wisdom, our intuition becomes blocked and ceases to function correctly. Our fear starts to feed our ego until we feel out of control in some way.

We find we feel better when we can control the outcomes of the little things, and this extends outwards into trying to control everything around you to feel safe.

Control is a problem for self-hate when:

- it makes you the bully. Why would anyone want you now?

- you can't relax, and no one enjoys being around that

- everything has to be perfect, so you can't tolerate if it isn't and you get lonely

- there's no spontaneity or joy, so you're boring

- you get out of control when people don't do it your way, so your behaviour is less attractive

Remedy for Control

Do the 'Daily Reset to Spirit' guided meditation from chapter three daily.

We seek to control because we fear being hurt in some way. If we protect ourselves by planning away the risk, or by making sure people can't really see you, everything will be okay.

So, the remedy for control is to look at your fear. When you master your fear, the risk falls away. When you heal your heart the reason to protect falls away. You start living a more intuitive and happy life. You can relax, enjoy and try something new.

Use the fear mastery techniques from earlier in the book and heal your heart using the guided meditation in chapter six to let go of the hurt in your past.

Deception

When you have lost the connection with your spirit, you start to focus upon your adequacies in an unhealthy way. You're internally terrified of being seen as inadequate, so you tell stories to avoid detection and to make you more interesting. When you are good at lying to yourself, you become excellent in seeing it in others. You mistakenly believe that you are failing or lacking in a very serious way.

Deception is a problem for self-hate when:

- they use sarcasm and it hurts because they're putting you down

- they lie and you know that they know that you know

- your lies are starting to trip you up and you're embarrassed

- you lie to make yourself feel better but end up feeling worse

- you lie to protect yourself and are disempowered as a result

- you lie to make yourself interesting which just makes you more of a loser

- you lie to hide just how pathetic you are and are ashamed

Remedy for Deception

Choosing to lie about yourself or your abilities or circumstances is creating undue clutter in your brain that you don't need. If it accumulates over time, it will either create an inability to concentrate and remember, or alternately it will interfere with your ability to see what is true. Your lies will become your truth, and you'll never realise just how fabulous you really are. The lies create a negative filter over your insight into what makes you good and great. It's like looking through muddy eye-glasses.

Master your fear of being seen for who you are, using the fear mastery techniques. Give yourself permission to be seen.

Take a big breath and be brave enough to tell the truth. If people don't like you for who you are, they are not your people. Keep practicing telling the truth of who you are and you'll find yourself drawing in your type of people.

Loneliness

Loneliness is a powerful symptom of having lost your natural connection with your spirit. You can't find or feed your own self-love, and it feels as if you've been deserted. Even those who appear to care about or love you can't fill that internal need. You may even doubt the truth of their love.

Loneliness is a problem for self-hate when:

- No one understands you

- No one has time for you

- You don't have people around you who are your sort of people

- You refuse to listen to the truth of the positive things said about you

- You isolate yourself or shut down from those who still care

- You believe the negative judgement or your inadequacy from the media

- You believe or create negative judgements in those that are around you

Remedy for Loneliness

The best and quickest remedy for loneliness is to stop and ask someone who you think would be truthful, and who actually likes you, to write down three good things about you. Sit with the piece of paper they've written on and breathe, breathe in the qualities and imagine them as yours. Imagine that you are becoming those things. Take a deep breath and ask yourself what else you can see that makes you nice or good or kind.

Ignore that negative voice in your head. Don't see it as the enemy, just allow yourself to be bored with its constant drone of saying the same things. Do what you do when you're bored—find something else to fill your time and engage your attention.

Practice meditation or get an energy healing or balance to reconnect you to your spirit. Use the first meditation track in this book. (Remember, you can download it for free!)

Actively look for your kind of people. Try everything once; a class or activity or a date or anything that gets you out meeting people. Breathe into your fear and do it anyway.

⌒

Wow! That's quite a list and it's only some of the most common emotions. There are so many variations of our experience, but this list is representative of them all in some form. It is true of each of the emotions we've described.

It's amazing to realise that experiences that have since become a non-issue, seeming so meaningless, still live in our body and have an affect even today. Your energy became blocked somewhere in response. Who could have imagined that sibling rivalry issues could still be limiting us now? When I began to notice the common themes in clients of my healing sessions and classes, I began to parent in a totally different way. I want my kids to know that they're good because they're good, not because of some over-inflated sense of importance or lack that results from me comparing them to a better behaved sibling or friend.

This self-hate information does not address behaviours that are 'wrong'. It looks solely at the emotions behind it. If you have done something 'wrong', you need to work closely to actively problem solve the outcomes. It's important to apologise and attempt to make amends for those times when you cause/create harm from a karmic perspective.

We know that we will reap what we sow, so it's very important to keep the energy output in a positive vibration. Making amends or trying to address it turns the vibration of the energy. Those affected may never forgive you for your part in it, and there's nothing you can do about that. It is not your job to fix their reactions to the experience.

It is your job to ensure that the sum total of positive energy you put out into the Universe is greater than that of the negative energy resulting from your attitudes, choices and behaviour.

Abandoning the Self-Criticism

The day I fell in love with Berni, marked the last day that I could live with this constant state of denial of my brilliance. It's possible I fell in love the moment I saw him; I just didn't know it as love. When I was with Berni I just felt whole, not lacking at all. Not only did I not feel inadequate when I was with him, he wouldn't tolerate any such talk. And then there was the 'Karina gazing'. It's pretty hard to continue to believe there's something wrong with you when you have a man staring at you with such palpable love, just because looking at you brings joy to his heart. It flew in the face of everything I had believed before.

Each day I'd look at my reflection in a mirror. Any woman will tell you there are 'great' mirrors and 'bad' mirrors. The great accentuate your great bits and you look fabulous in whatever you're wearing. The bad mirrors make everything you don't like look bigger and uglier. I've known people who refuse to shop in stores with 'bad' mirrors. When Berni came along, he smashed the 'bad' mirror that lived in my mind, and replaced it with a 'great' mirror. All of a sudden, I could see what wasn't real and I couldn't believe it. A long list of misconceptions were ready to be addressed.

My greatest misconception was that no one could ever love a girl like me. It sourced from my crooked teeth, glasses and shameful psychic ability. As I became single, I had to accept that I had numerous guys interested in me. I had choices, so it seemed lots of people could love me.

In addition to the men, I had plenty of people who loved me for my healing and psychic work. I could understand that love; for when someone gives you your life back or eliminates a significant issue or illness, you will always value their contribution. I was surrounded by beautiful people who were embracing my friendship, more than I had time for, so I could no longer support this belief. I let go of the story that made it true. In doing so, I became aware of the existence of *truth filters* in us all. When I worked with Debbie Ford in the USA and her book, *The Shadow Effect*, I became able to disempower them more quickly. I had a new insight and understanding that disintegrated the foundations of the beliefs that sourced my inadequacy and negativity.

All of a sudden, I was beginning to heal.

I had accumulated the most extraordinary amount of inaccurate beliefs, absorbed over the years, some of which would take decades to heal. Watching myself and my children, it became obvious how this had occurred. As young children, we are dependent upon our parent or our carers for our truth. As we reach our seventh birthday, our truth filters begin to develop, which enable us to digest our experiences in a different way.

We begin to question the truth of what we know or are told. If we have not experienced any sort of trauma, our filtering of the truth should develop normally. If we have known trauma, and it doesn't need to be massive, the development of our filters will be damaged. In some areas of your life, you will still see things through the eyes of a child, and this becomes fear's opportunity.

As I spent my days, weeks, months and years with Berni, my beliefs that had fallen through my damaged truth filters were challenged on an almost daily basis. I could no longer interpret my world in that way when he had awakened my reality.

This doesn't mean that I was childish or lacking maturity, in fact, quite the opposite. When our truth filters are even slightly damaged, we over-compensate so that no one can see. Very few of us walk with undamaged filters, and it is this that deceives us into believing we must become among those who are well-adjusted.

Those who appear to be the most well-adjusted on the outside, often have the worst and most inaccurate truth inside.

What's interesting is that once your truth filter is damaged, the belief that carries it will trigger every experience that it mirrors as you age. It's like our lack of ability to understand the reactions of others as a child created a story, such as 'no one will ever love you'. In the moment of hurt it seems true, and as time passes, a couple of experiences will prove the belief, and then the filter is set. Imagine being left out of a birthday party invitation or Mummy having another baby to replace you, and you can see where the misunderstanding can come from. Add into that a child's lack of ability to measure time, and things get bigger than they need to be very quickly.

Alas, what happens then, is that every situation has the ability to feed your beliefs and thus become your truth. Girls chatting in the playground admiring the way you do your pigtails could be falsely interpreted as 'they think I'm ugly, no one will ever love me now'. And there you have it. You've brought baggage into your 'now' that you probably can't even remember. When this occurs, our reactions become out of proportion to the situation, and we can be misinterpreted as unstable, overexcitable, highly needy or even unhinged.

Where my ex-husband would accuse me of overreacting, Berni would sit down with me to talk it through. We'd look at what this might stem from and define its truth. I had the insight to know that not all of my beliefs were real, yet my ego would use these beliefs as fuel to put me down.

I didn't want that experience to be in our relationship, so we supported each other to work through our own filters. I was shattered at the failure of my first marriage, particularly as I had tried so hard to make it work, to make him love me enough. Understanding my truth filter was damaged assisted me to not only heal my beliefs, but to begin using the insight for my clients.

Berni loved me so much, yet I felt like a fraud. I was entirely honest with him and held none of my failings back, and yet still he adored me. I would ask him what it was that made him love me over and over. A less secure man might have seen it as needy, but Berni could see that I was seeking my truth through his words.

I would turn them over and over and look within, until I could see them within myself. I felt guilty that I was so broken, yet he only saw the beauty in me. He couldn't understand why I thought I was a bad mother, when he so admired the parenting of my children and who they were becoming under my guidance. He couldn't understand why I thought I was a bad person, when I did so many wonderful things for so many people.

My centre of gravity was way off centre, yet I was so grateful for this opportunity to readjust how and where I saw myself in the world. And I found that he was right. The motivation born in my first marriage to heal everything that had stopped my ex-husband from loving me, had created a perfect platform to love and see who I was.

So, I chose to focus and expand on those things I knew I was good at. I focused on healing and teaching, and created courses which would evolve into what would later be renamed as Meliae Intuitive Healing. Despite those lingering thoughts that questioned my right to create a new healing modality, the results of my clients pushed them away. I was blown away every day by just how much my clients were shifting and changing their lives; physically, spiritually and mentally. Now my clients were pushing to be taught to heal like I was.

It was a tricky thing right from the start. I knew I was a great teacher, as the graduates of my first courses were constantly asking for more. I could heal so quickly and so well that people wanted those skills. I incorporated my nursing knowledge and taught basic anatomy and physiology, ethics, along with advanced healing techniques. They would learn everything in a weekend, and then go away to practice. I'd have them back a couple of months later to find that they too were incredible healers, who loved using this intuitive method of healing from the core instead of the symptoms.

I was getting busier and busier and struggling to fit everyone in. We decided to create an actual healing centre instead of me working from home. Initially I veered from my original vision when a friend offered to share the rooms to help out with expenses. My vision was one where all that I had discovered to be of benefit to profoundly heal myself and others, would be offered through the graduates from my courses. This would to help me manage an ever-increasing workload, yet I loved the idea of sharing costs and working with my friend.

Things came to a halt when I discovered I was pregnant, and after losing the baby, I lost myself in the grief. The healing centre could not be considered. As we had not yet told the children of the pregnancy, and believing it be an unnecessary grief, we kept the death of our baby a secret.

I was distraught in my unexpressed and hidden grief. I needed time to cry, so I headed to the mountains for a solo silent retreat.

And wow!

As I meditated on the porch of my cabin, I saw so much clarity. My belief in lack and desire to please meant that the core purpose of the centre had gone off track. I couldn't continue with my friend as a partner, and it broke my already fragile spirit to have to tell her. Again, my criticism of what a terrible friend I was amplified. I couldn't look at her, I felt like I had let her down and was so ashamed. I cared too much to hurt her, yet if I followed my spiritual guidance, that would have to be my path. I was devastated.

I've always had this conflict within me. I carry this deep knowing inside which people find hard to believe. I just know stuff, random stuff, and I don't know how or why. I know the waiter who just walked past me is grieving the loss of his grandfather, but I don't know him at all. I don't even need to check if this is fact—past experience proves my knowing true every time. I knew my new friend was pregnant or about to be the moment I sat next to her at a school function. My children had moved to the school when I moved in with Berni, and meeting the parents at this social function seemed like a great plan, until the inevitable question came up. "What do you do Karina?"

Those questions always end up in either an uncomfortable silence or, in this case, super excitement. "Ooooh, what can you see in me?" I looked at Sarah and told her what I could see. She laughed the pregnancy off, not wanting to embarrass me. She pulled me aside at the end of the night and quietly told me she had an IUD so she couldn't be pregnant. She had a kind, pitying expression on her face, but I stayed firm. "I've been doing this for a long time and I'm rarely wrong."

She left on a family holiday the next morning and two days later was in the emergency department. She told them there was no chance she was pregnant so they moved on to look at other causes. Despite the IUD, she was pregnant and critically ill.

As they walked away, she couldn't get my words out of her head. She called the nurse back and told her of my prediction, telling them that by all accounts I was good. She asked them to check.

They told her later that if she hadn't done so, or had come to the hospital half an hour later, she would have died. They'd eliminated pregnancy. The new urgent order on the pregnancy test saved her life, as Sarah had suffered a ruptured ectopic pregnancy.

I just knew she was pregnant. I could see the baby's soul. Nothing could change my mind. Luckily, Sarah had sat next to me at dinner and was strong enough to stand up with weird information. Our weekly breakfast gatherings would be so much less without her there.

Strength and faith are incredible qualities I really admire. I was watching the movie *Hidden Figures* not long ago, which is the true story of the black women who were instrumental in getting a man into orbit, and later to the moon, through NASA. Their struggle against ostracism was managed in the conviction that their skin colour did not represent their intelligence. The women were so strong and brave, but Katherine Johnson was particularly inspiring. She just knew what she knew. Math was dependable and never lied. She had such faith in its reliability that she could confidently send a man into space, knowing he could be retrieved.

That's how I feel about my gift. Regardless of what people think of me, I know what I know. I knew my husband's company would successfully achieve three massive takeovers at a time when the courts shut everything down. When I told Berni, he smiled and said, "I hope so love, but that would take a miracle at this point." Three miracles later as we stood at the celebration, others shaking their heads that I could have predicted it as true. I just know what I know.

I started out trying to be the perfect daughter. I wanted my parents to be proud of me, to see a good person with a good heart. Then as I grew, I wanted to be the perfect granddaughter who would help others in need, caring like Nanny did about people. Understanding and being able to see the future and into people meant I was super aware of when I'd upset, irritated or offended someone. I tried not to be that person. I tried to be the perfect person so that I wouldn't create disappointment. When I failed, it was physically painful inside, so I'd push that pain downwards into my belly. I got angry and frustrated at myself for not being perfect, and for the enormity of the pain it caused inside me.

When others didn't listen to or believe in me, I started to doubt what I knew, yet it was insistent. Me knowing is like being hungry. There's no possibility that your body isn't hungry and in the same way, there's no possibility that I don't know. I just need to be still and listen. I didn't understand that often I knew things to enable outcomes to be changed.

Being perfect then evolved into a 'thing'. I couldn't bear it when things weren't done right. As a nurse, you know that precision is key when you take blood or give an injection. Everything in my life was supporting this need for perfection. Then my need for perfection evolved into a 'control' thing. Nursing taught me that if you plan and watch and are careful, your patients can survive even life-threatening circumstances. The more organised you were and the more you knew or did, the more you could cope with emergencies. As emergencies were common, this quickly became an ingrained behaviour. It's no surprise that it overflowed into my day to day life. If you control the circumstances, you have more control over the outcomes of the events.

As a nurse, my knowing was a gift. I could feel or see people deteriorating before their bodies showed the signs, and many people's lives were saved or critical situations prevented or minimised because of this. I was on high alert all the time at the hospital, despite trying to avoid being openly psychic in my personal life. It's probably what saved me in the end, as I couldn't shut it down completely if I wanted to ensure my patients didn't die like Nanny.

I watched and found that I could find things in people's bodies on admission, which would later be confirmed through testing or surgery. Being a large referral and teaching hospital, I got to see things most medicos and nurses have never seen in person. I'd head home to my books and see pictures that matched what I could perceive in the body. It was incredible.

At the same time, my healing hands were amplifying and I found I had no control on when the warmth of the healing would spread through them. I'd be palpating a wound or placing my hand over an area of pain and patients were starting to react more often than not. They'd grab my hand and tell me not to move it, I was taking away their pain! I knew I had a magic there, and it would evolve into healing training, and I ensured I was perfect in that too! Eventually it was the ability in my hands that would take me away from the job I loved as a nursing manager. The money I earned could not be more important than using those hands.

My 'knowing' has got us out of tricky situations, prevented numerous disasters, avoided terrible traffic, and even saved me over $400 on a pair of designer shoes! That same knowing has reliably pulled me through the challenges of my life, always showing me how I end up when I'm through it. In the end, it was my intuition that enabled me to abandon my self-criticism. I didn't want to live like this anymore. I knew I was a magnet for my own experience. What I was putting out into the world, I knew I would get back. If I eliminated the conflict within me, I would not attract conflict and criticism from others. I wanted a life of ease and this meant I needed to change it from within first.

When I created my 'Make A Change A Day' recipe, it literally changed my life. Every day when I was up to it, I chose to let go of an old belief that had passed by my damaged truth filters. One by one they went: not a good enough nurse, or lover, or girlfriend, or wife, or friend, or provider, or manager, or business woman, or bookkeeper, or marketer, or—

The list went on forever. I still work on releasing old and limiting beliefs now. Those beliefs also extended into lack of belief in what I can achieve. This is not the first book I've written, just the first one I've published. I had to heal my belief that I wasn't a good enough author!

Publishing this or any book that talks about my experiences as a younger me is a perfect stimulator of self-criticism. Straight away, I'm thinking of how those featured in the book will take what I'm writing. But that really isn't any of my business. I've been told on many an occasion that I should write a book like no one will read it, and then it will speak to the hearts of the reader. That's all very well and good when people you care about still have to walk a journey with their story on display. I'm choosing to write my story, and as a contributor to my story, I can't leave anyone out. Most of what I have written has implications further than me, and I can hear the self-criticism rising.

Yet why should I not tell **my** story? I have carried the pain of my experiences and my beliefs for decades. Shouldn't I expect some sort of support and compassion for what has been a difficult and challenging life so far? Yet the reality is that not everyone will feel that way, and that is why I've kept it hidden for so long. Bit by bit I've gained the courage to share my stories with my clients and students to enable them to fast-track their healing. Often when we hear of another walking the same path as we've walked or are walking, it opens us up to insights or enables our past difficulties to heal and dissipate. I'm not proud of everything I've done in life, I don't think any of us are. Most of us have our secrets buried deep inside.

Don't each of us deserve to have our story heard, to be supported through the hard times. Shouldn't we have the space to revisit traumas to heal without being ostracised? Don't *you* deserve the space to work through your challenges as you are facing them, and receive kindness and support. Isn't that what community is? I'm hoping your community rallies around you as you heal. As for me, I know I'll face criticism, but it will never be as harsh or as damaging as that I've had for myself. Nothing can hurt me that much ever again.

I think of my parents and I hope they are not interpreting my story as a criticism of their role in my life. They have been perfect for what I have needed to develop. I know my parents love me and that they have done the best they could with a child with such extraordinary needs. Being a parent myself, I know we all look back in retrospect and see how we would do it now.

We walk this journey together.

I didn't come with an instruction book and neither did my children. We are all doing the best we can with what we know at the time. I know at times I have failed my children and I wish it wasn't so.

I think despite the very best of intentions, all parents do.

I firmly believe that the best parents are those that love their children, who are not afraid to say 'no' when their child's feelings might be hurt, and who keep close boundaries around behaviour. Those things keep children feeling safe.

My parents did all of that and provided for us pretty well, considering their lack of income after Dad's accident when I was twelve. They kept their marriage mostly together and their kids have all grown up valuing family. We love catching up whenever we're in the same part of the country!

My parents didn't fail me. They made me who I am; for all that they gave to me and for all that they couldn't or wouldn't. I didn't like them for all of it and I was certainly a very normal and moody teenager. But when I had cancer, there was no mistaking the enormity of their love for me. Despite the fact that I was a tricky child, they did a good job and I couldn't be more grateful for all of it, good and bad.

I try to remind myself of that when I feel that I could/should have done more as a parent for our children. I know I'm not always ticking the boxes of their ideal life, yet what I do know is that none of them lack in love. Sometimes I feel as though I might burst with the enormity of the love I have when I see or think of them.

One thing I am good at is loving people. When Berni talks to me about how I parented, he would often say how blown away he was with how much I loved our children. With how much I loved his children. When I married him, he came as a package with a teenager and a pre-teen. Not their best time of life to merge in a new family, yet there was no question that I could take on him without loving his children. When I said yes to him, I was saying yes to his children. I chose them as my own, in the same way you do when you choose to get pregnant. I was not going to have kids living in my house who weren't loved as much as my children, or who were treated as less or inferior in any way.

So, despite not giving birth to them (thanks Lauren!), I get to have an extra son and daughter and love them. Merging families is no picnic and there were plenty of opportunities to continue that pattern of criticising myself, but I chose not to. I can't tell you how hard that is when you've got grumpy teenagers and small children and the washing is mounting in the laundry! I would see the pain of missing their other parent, or the difficulties they were all experiencing through the separations and living between two homes, and so I would just love them more. It was all I could do. I couldn't take away their experience, but I could try to love and nurture away their pain.

I would focus upon what I was good at and spend time on that. I ignored (or tried to) the critical voice inside my head every time she spoke. I started to see that voice like a complaining, rude, and at times, naughty child. I started to talk to her as I would to my children. I knew I was better at raising good children than I was at loving and supporting myself, so I saw that voice as another child and called her Isabelle.

Isabelle was out of control and needed to learn some manners!

"No, stop being so negative!"

"Only one person speaks at a time and right now that's me."

"Ugh! Stop it, if you haven't got anything nice to say, don't say anything at all."

And so, it would go. I knew I was good at forgiveness, so I worked on that too. I focused on looking at every person who had disappointed, hurt, rejected, abandoned or offended me in some way. I saw their experience from their side of things and I let it all go. This was bigger than forgiving as I had a memory that could regurgitate whole conversations word for word. I refused to carry around the pain of their behaviour, particularly when many of them would struggle to remember or care about something that had happened so long ago. Friendship, relationship and workplace issues as both a teen and an adult slid away, and all of a sudden, I was so much less critical of myself.

Then I worked on forgiving me. Wow, was that hard! I was the one person that should have known better. Yet, I have to admit that it's way easier being a psychic and healer and seeing into the world, its people and their energy. Being a person has meant I have had to feel ... and I hate it.

I hate the pain.

I hate the hurt and I can't always figure things out. I can't imagine why someone would become less of themselves to make someone else happy, yet I have done that. I can't imagine why someone would lie and make themselves look bad rather than hurt someone's feelings, yet I have done that. I can't imagine why you would forget that you came with a plan; to feel that which you couldn't where we came from, yet I have done that.

When I think about my experience, it hurts because I fail to remember sometimes that we are all the same. We are all souls who come from the most brilliant place, which I miss every day. We are made of that same incredible energy. When I look at someone, that is what I see—the brilliance of their spirit. It's so bright and so beautiful and so perfect that I am almost brought to tears when I see that they cannot see it at all. I realise now that the years where I could not see my own brilliance were the years that brought me the most pain.

Yet I did not walk this journey alone, along the way I have had people in every year of my life who are there to remind me that I am so brilliant too. I call them my angels, yet many others have been my teachers by creating the hardship I've known. They have created the challenge to become so brilliant. I'm grateful to them all and for the guidance of my angels and guides too.

I've worked out that I'm not alone, even when I'm by myself.

When I love myself enough, I feel so loved and full and perfect and happy that I don't need anyone else. When I feel like that, I can't wait to find others to share my love and my joy with, yet I'm just as happy on my own. I try to live in a way that will make the older version of me proud when she looks back.

Life is enough for me now, and cancer has continued to teach me that in a way that cannot be ignored. It has shown me that I should use my story to help others, to see that our way of loving ourselves is sick.

I want to show people how full and wonderful their life could be if they just loved themselves first.

Meditation: Loving Self

D o this meditation initially every day to nurture your spirit. Read or speak it slowly, with pauses at the end of sentences. Take yourself to a quiet space where you'll not be interrupted for a while. Turn off your phone, close the door and get yourself comfortable.

Taking some nice big deep breaths ... slowly now ... just breathing nice and deep and slow.

You are aware of your body and are aware of the sounds in the room as you breathe.

And as you breathe, you are focusing upon those same sounds until they fade away.

You can just hear my voice now, everything else has faded into the background.

You, are beginning to feel ever so relaxed.

Breathing even deeper, your breathing is becoming slow.

You are becoming even more relaxed.

As you breathe, you bring your focus to the area around your forehead between the eyebrows.

You imagine your breath can breathe here.

Breathe into this space.

Imagine now that you are lifting your awareness away from the room, away from your body.

Imagine or create a feeling in your mind that you can see a gently flowing stream or river.

The water is clear today and trickling by.

At the side of the river there is a soft cushion of soft, soft grass.

You are drawn to this patch of grass and settle yourself down.

It's the perfect height for you to dangle you toes or fingers in the water.

The water is refreshing, the perfect antidote to your warm and tired feet.

As you sit there, you find this place feels ever so safe, you are becoming ever so relaxed.

It's so quiet with just the sounds of the breeze and the water trickling by.

Sometimes you'll hear the call of a bird.

So, it's quite a surprise when you hear a very young voice say hello.

You look to your right and see a young child sitting by you, who is the spitting image of you as a child.

You're so surprised you find words are not there, so you smile gently, remembering who you were at that age.

The child is indeed a younger version of you, and through some magic in the air of this place, has appeared to help you now.

You see in this child, and perhaps even remember, just how little you were and how confusing or perplexing the world was.

You feel drawn to comfort and love this child, so you gently say hello.

The child understands who you are, but is feeling uncertain, in need somehow.

You ask the child, "how old are you?" and smile gently at the response.

"You know little one, things might seem scary right now, but things really do get better.

Look at me, I'm big now and I'm okay ... everything worked out and I'm okay.

I know that you get scared sometimes, but that's just cause you're too little to see or too young to understand.

You know that I love you little one, I will do anything to make sure you stay safe.

You don't need to worry anymore."

You notice the sense of wanting to believe, but not being entirely sure. You realise this littler version of you is missing something to make it easier.

"Little one, what do you need to be safe?"

You listen, watch or feel closely for this child's response.

You know it inside you or can perceive it directly from the child.

Your heart opens wider and goes out to the child.

The bigger, more grown version of you understands how little it will take, to make a difference.

You tell the child you will and are surprised as the child jumps up to give you a hug.

As you go to hug the child, you realise the child is no longer there, the child has become you once more.

You feel such love for the little one that was once you, and it starts you to thinking.

If my little one needed something so small to feel safe, what about the now version of me?

So, you breathe deeply, and you begin to listen, and you ask yourself.

"What, my dear one, do you need to feel safe? What do you need to feel loved?"

You listen, watch or feel closely for a soft and loving response.

If it doesn't come straight away, you breathe deeper and deeper and wait again.

You know it inside you or can perceive it through thoughts, words, memories or feelings.

Your heart opens wider and goes out to the part of you that isn't feeling safe.

The wise part of you understands how little it will take to make a difference.

You make a commitment to give to yourself, that which you need to feel safe and loved.

You feel surprised at the wave of love that washes through you.

Your arms naturally rise and enfold you as you embrace you.

A small and simple change that could make all the difference pops into your head.

You feel excited and motivated to put this change in place now.

You know that small changes, when joined together, change your reality and you're excited for what the changes will bring.

You feel fears rise and disappear as the love and certainty in the change take charge.

You know now that everything will indeed be okay.

Your heart is expanding, and its natural intelligence is expanding to assist you to make the change with ease and grace.

You feel such love and joy now.

Life is so full of possibility, you're excited.

You know now that you are a beautiful person, you're not sure how it happened. You suspect it had something to do with your heart intelligence.

You feel this overwhelming sense of love and kindness towards you and ready yourself to be more understanding and patient of your journey here.

As your awareness of the room and its sounds return to you, you feel the same love and joy and kindness seeping through every part of your body.

You breathe it in with delight.

As you open your eyes, you enjoy some water and feel such hope for the future, you instinctively know all will be well.

You rise and return to your day or snuggle down to sleep, knowing that you will return to this meditation often, as you can see it is feeding your soul.

Loving Myself Enough to Write

It's a few minutes to midnight on the last night of the worst and best year of my life. We are known for our annual New Year's Eve party. Our house is filled with so much joy and love. The DJ from the 'Bye-Bye Tessie' party is back and the house is pumping. It's a much smaller party and I'm so grateful to spend precious time with these special friends. Not everyone could make it, but I can feel them here anyway.

What a year it's been. We could never have imagined its enormity or what it would mean for us a year ago. We had hoped for a year that would bring great love, happiness and success. As I look around the people dancing, chatting and playing darts, I can see the joy there. While we would never have wanted it in this way, the year has delivered. Our relationships with so many people have deepened, and I'm not the only survivor. Waz survived his massive heart attack earlier in the year so there's much to celebrate.

There's no greater way to measure success than to have life after cancer.

The joy and the love that came from beating one of the rarest cancers is immeasurable. Knowing that I did it my way, without compromising what I believe in is even better. I know that the medical world does not consider it cured, and that's okay. I know I will never see it again.

I will never again need it.

I'm so much healthier, and managing my energy and capacity to give really well most days. I'm focused on improving my self-care and know that my vibrancy is expanding every day.

The countdown is on. I'm dancing on the dancefloor in a new dress and I couldn't be happier to see in 2017!

10 ... 9 ... 8 ... 7 ... 6 ... 5 ... 4 ... 3 ... 2 ... 1 ... Happy New Year!

Berni has me in his arms and the tears in his eyes match mine. "Happy New Year, beautiful. I love you so, so, so much!"

I kiss him so hard and tell him I love him and thank him for everything. "I could never have done it without you, you are my everything!"

Not all of our children are here, but I send them all so much love and thank them silently for their support and for being mine. Then I'm being pulled away as everyone is kissing and hugging me and wishing me the best ever year.

As the last people leave, we clean up the entire party. We've had offers to help but we are grateful for the opportunity to just soak in the ability to be together and to send our love energy so fully into the New Year ahead and the future. We have to pack up everything as we're heading back to Hawaii in the morning.

We wake to a happy family and a clean house—now that's a New Year's first! It's already got the vibes of a fabulous year ahead. We spend the day packing up the Christmas tree and decorations, sorting out the ice buckets and packing.

Before we've finished, the car is there to whisk us to the airport. We're running late, but we don't care. Having brunch with the kids is way more important. We chuck everything in and hope it's all there. If not, Hawaii has plenty of everything!

We've decided that we're visiting just two of our favourite islands of Hawaii to ensure a relaxing and healing experience. We've had a hell of a year and we're both emotionally and physically exhausted.

This time it's just Zavier and the two of us and he's not travelled exceptionally well. He's missing our dog and his siblings terribly, so there have been tears. All of a sudden, allowing him to be up till 2 am is looking like a poor choice, but it is what it is.

Hawaii weaves it's magic and soon enough there's laughter and fun everywhere.

We've gone all out to celebrate as Berni wants to spoil me; there's nothing more exciting to him than celebrating my life. The Four Season's Hotel is definitely spoiling me, and have thought of every little detail. The resort is beachfront with three restaurants, a bar, an awesome pool and our room has a large balcony overlooking the ocean. This place is gorgeous and the food is fantastic too, with healthy kids meal options at each restaurant!

I'm wearing my one-piece bathers with matching sarong to protect my scar from the sun, and the beautiful designs of Australian designer Camilla are making me feel beautiful too.

We're waiting to board our boat to go whale watching. After our incredible experiences with the dolphins and manta rays, we're keen to see the majestic energy of the whales, if only from a distance. I'm standing on the boat laughing, holding my hat and watching Berni with his camera and massive lens.

Everyone is excited and we aren't disappointed, the whales are out to play. We watch from a distance, but I can feel their energy from the boat. After a while, we stop the boat and drop a microphone in the water to listen to their song.

I stand with tears in my eyes, there is such majesty and love in their music. Their music is said to heal and I can feel the vibration of their song through my whole body. I stand very still while recording it, to breath it all in. You can hear the majesty of these incredible animals and it almost feels like a highly spiritual sound. This is an experience to remember.

We spend most of our time, apart from our whale trip, at the resort. It's just so fabulous, why would we want to go anywhere else? Days around the pool lazing in our cabana while getting spa treatments and food and drinks brought to us is the ultimate remedy for the year we've had. Berni and Zavier try out their new full face snorkels and play catch in the pool, often drawing a crowd of kids together. This is great for Zavier as he's often shy about mixing without a sibling for courage. I'm actually reading my magazines and books!

It is so lovely to just take time out without worry or guilt that I need to be addressing other things. I know the dog and the business are okay, and I hope the other kids are old enough to stay out of mischief. That may be debatable with two of them housesitting, but if I don't think about it, it's like I don't even have a house. I am just so relaxed.

I even agree to go zip lining up near the crater of the mountain. To be upfront with you, I'd have to say that while we had previously zip lined in Fiji, it was not my most favourite activity. Zavier, on the other hand loved it, and couldn't get enough.

We traipse up the mountain, not on foot, thankfully, but in an ATV. I'm sure you can feel my reluctance through these pages. The idea of propelling myself through the air in a harness that is not always comfortable, on nothing more than a wire and some clips, seems less than wise. Yet this is the new me, the one who promised herself on the last trip to live without fear and limits, so off we go.

As we travel around the course, I watch a mum of a couple of teenage kids fight her terror of heights to complete the course with them. She is incredible, I wish I could remember her name to give her credit, because I look at her and see real fear.

I look at myself and see a woman who likes to control her outcomes.

On that basis, I choose to let go of any reluctance or fear and start to love the exhilaration of the wind in my face as I speed along over spectacular valleys and bushland. It is time to really start living. I am alive and I want every day to count. I spoil myself and eat the lobster at Hawaii's best restaurant as a reward. If I'm going to be really living, then I'm living it to the full!

Before we are ready, it is time to leave my beloved Maui and head to Honolulu on Oahu. After the Four Seasons, we know few hotels could measure up to the incredible service and special attention we've all individually received there. We stay at the Halekulani which is considered one of the island's best hotels. Alas it was nowhere near as kid friendly and the boys weren't allowed to play catch with their ball. Their routine of fun was broken, so we sought other things to do. Of course, there is shopping, so not all is lost. I love to bring home pressies for the kids left at home whenever I travel. I make sure that I support the Hawaiian economy and buy some treasures to take away.

I love to watch Ellen TV online and am inspired by her generosity and willingness to just be the brilliance of herself, despite the societal resistance around gay women. I watched her clips in hospital and throughout my recovery. She always spoke to me of courage and being true to herself. As I spent time watching her in Hawaii, it was becoming apparent that I needed to step up and finally start to teach globally if that was my dream.

It is, I want to help people all over the globe, yet I am shy of how I will be received.

Who am I to teach others to be happy? As we travel through Hawaii, I think of Ellen and realise that if she had cared about what people thought of her when she came out, she'd not be doing the incredible work she does each and every week.

I am feeling so inspired that I agree to book us into a massive zip lining experience where we'll be traveling over massive valleys of 730 m/2400 ft at speeds of around 112 km/70 miles an hour.

What am I thinking?

Well, I think of Ellen and her courage, and I create a challenge for myself. If I can do this course and all it demands of me (within reason, as my body was still recovering) I will start my book. I will put myself out there and speak to those who will listen. I will teach them to love themselves enough to put their joy first, to shine the true brilliance of who they are.

As I stand at the top of swaying platforms on what seems to be massive mountains, overlooking the tiny looking ocean, I am tempted to head back into my old way of 'doing' life. But I know I've survived for a reason, so I take a deep breath and whisper to myself, "That is my old pattern, I'm choosing to do it a different way today and every day after."

I launch myself into the nothingness, miles over the treetops, and embrace the joy of it.

I realise I have the recipe now—when I focus upon the joy, there is no fear!

I am ready to write and the ten days in Hawaii have given me the opportunity to love myself enough to actually do it. Berni's generosity and love has buoyed me into mirroring his love with my own. We celebrate, overlooking the ocean with a degustation dinner at La Mer. Zavier spends most of his time looking at his iPad between meals, and we spend all of it looking into each other's eyes with such love. I am truly the luckiest and most loved girl in the world. I am ready.

I start writing things down.

Action!
Creating New Habits: A New You!

"They always say time changes things,
but you actually have to change them yourself."
—*Andy Warhol*

C hange is the only thing that you can be sure of in life. Nothing is ever entirely the same: not the date, time, location, weather, people, actions, beliefs and your feelings. How you woke up today was different to how you woke up on every other morning of your life. No other day had the experience or knowledge or skills that you had or gained yesterday. The only thing with change being constant is that nothing is ever the same, and this has just become your best friend. You can use this to your advantage.

Every day you can consciously make changes and improvements to your experience. Or not.

It's your choice, your future.

You can choose to have an attitude where you put yourself in the driver's seat of your destiny, and choose driving forward into a life where the only constant **is** change. This way has no rules and nothing will be routine, but your destiny will be fuelled by your joy and care for yourself. You will be attracting success, love and joy each and every day. You'll be happy!

Or you can choose to drive in reverse, and live through the mistakes and errors of your past, marking them as the road directions on your destiny map. You can expect that things will continue mostly the same. You'll still live in fear, doubt yourself and be critical enough at times to prevent your true brilliance attracting an incredible future. The beliefs you held in the past will continue to define how you see yourself tomorrow and all the tomorrows after.

I chose to change and I'm ever so happy for it now, but I won't pretend it wasn't hard work. Think of how many years you've spent defining your now. The process of undoing the limits and lack and dimming of your brilliance of your past will take time.

That's why this book is not just a story.

That's why you are walking away with the tools and guided meditations with the healing already embedded, to ensure you can create your own success. Of course, if I saw you in person I could accelerate your progress, but there's nothing more fabulous than the looking back and knowing that you've done it yourself.

All of my methods of healing and teaching have always focused on *you* being in charge of recreating your destiny. This is no different.

Here's another one of my master recipes for success.

New Habits for a New You!

- The strengths of self-love

- Actions of self-love

- Words of kindness

- Acts of kindness

- Small acts of kindness

- Daily evaluations to ensure kindness prevails

- Forgiving your failings

- Accepting your path as a student of life

- Allowing the difficulty in the unfamiliarity and just do it anyway!

Breaking the habits of being yourself is just that easy, but did you know that you can break this down one down further? Here's my recipe for each one individually.

The Strengths of Self-Love

Understand that if you feed yourself, you can never be hungry. You can never need to look to someone or something or somewhere that does not honour your highest good. Think of a way of living that doesn't include the need to recriminate yourself for your choices. You'll walk to a really happy place when you feed yourself first. You never feel like you're too depleted to assist where it's appropriate to do so.

Actions of Self-Love

To truly love yourself, you must take time to feed and fuel your body well. Feed it fresh and healthful food and water, exercise, sleep, stimulation, meditation, silence, creativity, passion, interactions with others, connection with your chosen family and opportunities to learn and support yourself. Then feed yourself love through touch and play. Seek ways to massage and soak your body in love, imagine massaging your skin with oil or soaking in the ocean or a bath. Seek ways to infuse joy into everything you do, you must find at least five laughs a day. Imagine watching funny clips on YouTube if you're a bit short on giggles.

Words of Kindness

Speak to yourself with words that show you respect who and what you are as a soul. Know you have great purpose, even if it doesn't seem apparent or important to you. Know you have come to this planet to make a difference in your own special way. Allow yourself the time and space to learn the knowledge and skills required to develop the wisdom you need to make a difference. Speak kindly to yourself with both your words and your thoughts. Be ever watchful.

Acts of Kindness

Look for ways to be kind to you. Give yourself permission to make mistakes. Have patience as you watch yourself evolve and grow into today's new version of you. You have time to be who and what you need to be. Know that the best path does not always end up being what you might see as the most direct path. Allow yourself to be guided by your highest wisdom by listening to the quiet and loving voice of your intuition. When you trust yourself and life, you are kind to your every outcome.

Small Acts of Kindness

Giving to others in moderation is such a great gift, but only when it honours them to do so. Ask yourself if it honours them for you to do this. If it does, go right ahead. If it does not, then seriously think about your reasons for doing this for them. Are you willing, knowing it is taking away their opportunities to learn, and that the lesson must return again, in an amplified way to ensure it gets learned? Allow them to be the best they came here to be. Help if you're asked, but help by showing and empowering them to do it themselves. A good mentor is worth a million servants. Ensure you are the mentor making a difference. Use your brilliance to teach theirs.

Daily Evaluations to Ensure Kindness Prevails

Measure yourself each day for your successes. Ignore what you haven't as yet done. While there is life there is time. The most important deadlines are flexible, and the unimportant ones don't matter. They're unlikely to be remembered or matter ten years down the track. Look to your wins and focus upon what you're good at. Use your skills to create the success you need, and outsource or seek extra help or training to turn your weaknesses into your new strengths. Remember that everything you're now good at was once a weakness.

Forgiving your Failings

Getting something wrong is not a failing. It is a step towards getting it right. You didn't learn to ride a bike or walk the first time you tried it, so quit expecting success on every try. It's cruel. If you would forgive a very small child or someone you cared about who was dying for this weakness or mistake, forgive yourself. While you continue to learn, you live here. When you tick off everything on your learning life list, you die. Start living and let go of your failings. They do not define you any more than a child who falls down while learning to walk. We all get it eventually!

Accepting your Path as a Student of Life

Your job here is to experience what you can't experience in the place you came from. Each time you learn, when you heal and let go, you raise your vibration. Each time you do that, you have become smart or wise enough to learn some more. Don't see each challenge or drama or trauma as a bad thing. You are getting to do this because you have excelled at your last level of learning. Applaud the brilliance of who you are, and focus upon what you need to learn, gain or attain to allow this lesson to be mastered too.

Allowing the Difficulty in the Unfamiliarity and Just Do It Anyway!

The one thing about change is that it is always uncertain. There is nothing that allows any of us the comfort of staying the same, that can create more goodness, joy, love and success in your life. There is nothing to be gained in staying the same. So be brave, take a breath and just do it anyway. If you don't get it right, change something else: your attitude, actions or beliefs and try again. Each time you do, your brain makes new pathways. Each time you don't your brain clears away old things you don't need. You forget to enable space to create mastery in the new.

♡ *Just Do It!* ♡

No More Limits

When I created the Flying Souls Institute of Healing, I placed myself onto the most ridiculously steep learning curve. I knew nothing about business, a bit about budgeting and enough about managing people to think I'd be alright. How wrong that turned out to be.

We opened the centre thinking that it would grow really fast, as the locals joined my already extensive list of clients who loved the results of Meliae Intuitive Healing. I employed my graduates, massage therapists, and my bridesmaid, Fran, to manage the administration. I'd given Fran a job when she was retrenched, to work through my backlog of admin. She managed it and helped with creating the centre while I was pregnant and managing our renovation. It seemed a natural progression to choose her for the role.

I had just brought home my precious little baby boy, and I was struggling to manage the workload. We employed a nanny, furnished a large nursery for the three younger children onsite to enable me to breastfeed on demand, and a housekeeper for a few months to prevent me from drowning in housework. Berni was working long hours and having the extra help was a lifesaver.

If I'd thought I knew what running a business would be like, I could never have anticipated the stress that would come with long hours and trying to make the finances balance. Everywhere I turned, someone needed or wanted something from me; from a cuddle or a feed, to a clean shirt or uniform, to decisions on policy and ordering. I learnt by listening to my intuition most of the time. When I didn't, I failed. When I listened, things went well. Still I was way too tired to manage the stillness required to function intuitively. I had good days and bad.

A few months later when the Global Financial Crisis (GFC) hit, our surrounding suburbs and potential clientele went from being very affluent to struggling. Children were pulled out of private schools, houses and cars were sold and stress was everywhere. Our ability to pull new clients from those who could benefit most disappeared overnight. No one had the confidence to spend extra when tomorrow it might not be there. Then there were those who had no extra in the first place.

I had employed a heap of staff and my projections relied on income being generated by all of our therapists. The building we had leased for the centre was huge, we even had a massive internal fairy garden for the kids to run around inside. All of a sudden, I couldn't justify the wages of my staff, yet there were single mums or sole earners among them. Jointly, Berni and I decided that as we had the luxury of being very comfortable, we would keep them on. There were people going under everywhere, and we cared too much to see them suffer.

That GFC was the longest that I remember having. It seemed that people lost their ability and confidence in the future. It took a long time to recover and still we didn't have the heart to let people go.

Before we knew it, we had invested hundreds of thousands of dollars in Flying Souls and our personal financial situation was compromised. Companies we had invested in went bankrupt, and combined with our investments in the staff of Flying Souls, we were now looking at a very different financial story. My stress went through the roof. I had no idea how to trade away our debts and felt so guilty that I'd used so much of our money.

I asked the angels for help, to provide us with assistance if we were meant to continue the work of the centre. The abundance came, and as I worked on manifesting, it came over and over and over again. Despite the assistance, we decided that running a business with such a huge staff was taking too great a toll on me, and we had to downsize. Many staff left and with them went such disappointment. I loved working and sharing my life with these people, and I felt like I had failed.

The new location was beachside, in a shopping strip and right near the train station. It could not be more perfect. We began a whole new way of functioning and found the smaller team created a camaraderie and intimacy that was lacking before. Di took over running the administration and allowed me the space to focus upon treating and teaching. Berni's business was taken over, we bought a new house and things were looking great. Zavier was at a fabulous new school and we were so impressed that we moved Maddie and Lachy there too. At the time, we had lots of personal challenges in people we loved and were close to, but on the whole things were so much better than before. I had worked on everything that was creating stress by destroying the limits that each situation or relationship imposed.

Our lives were the happiest that they'd ever been. Our kids were happy, Maddie graduated school well, Lachy was halfway through his final year of school and both Dylan and Elyse were working and in relationships with lovely partners. Everyone seemed to be pretty happy. We were planning a holiday with the inheritance from Berni's Mum to Hawaii with all of the kids. It was a magical and happy time.

But I was tired all of the time. I had years of anaemia so I didn't find it odd. I had an episode of severe abdominal pain a couple of years earlier, but the CT scans were all clear. Just a pesky endometrial growth to heal when I had time. I was so, so busy. I had no time for anything, let alone me.

I'd seen a doctor to investigate my tiredness and my iron levels were seriously low. I had to have an iron infusion, but prior to that I needed a gastroscopy and colonoscopy to ensure nothing was wrong. My procedures went well and I had the iron infusion.

Initially after recovering from a problem with near anaphylaxis, my energy had returned.

But that was a year ago. Maybe it was time to get another infusion, but I'm allergic to it. I thought I'd make an appointment with the doctor when I have the time. I was so tired I couldn't even make it through the day. I was getting fatter and fatter and nothing appeared to help. I'd put away the photos of our trip to Paris to renew our wedding vows the year before, because my stomach looked so big. I should get to the gym more often, if only I could find the energy.

I woke up one busy morning so pleased to have a myotherapy session for my very painful shoulder. I had no idea that day would change the rest of my life, that I would find a large mass under my ribs on the left side of my abdomen. I could not have imagined that the next day I would be diagnosed with cancer. Life was finally going so well ...

A New Beginning ...
Shining Brightly

As I recovered from cancer, I started to see how I could empower my ability to be happier and healthier every day. I see my patterns and I'm back in charge. As soon as I see them, I interrupt their flow by choosing differently or taking a different tack.

I am ready to support myself and I can see the times when fear, doubt or guilt have its way with me. I notice when I'm tired, upset, hungry, sad, unwell, grieving, or stressed and I've designed strategies to deal with those times. Now they are no longer my weaknesses and I'm once again back in charge of my destiny.

I've been listening to my heart and I'm using the ability to work with healing energy and the intelligence of the heart to create health and wellbeing in myself and others. I've been creating healing in others like this since I was a little girl, but now I do it faster. It's so fast and so powerful that I need to be careful of overdoing it. I'm really aware of my tendency to do too much and I'm constantly putting brakes on my enthusiasm, to match it to my ability to actually do it.

The one thing I've been amazed at was the limits of my body. Once I'd healed and recovered and relaxed, I committed to only work within the comfortable level of energy expenditure of my body. Wow, was I doing way too much before!

Berni's mum was a mother of six in the times where women did everything, and did it without the benefits of machines and technology like we do. She'd watch me in my life or at work when she visited for treatment and shake her head. She'd tell me often that she had no idea how I was doing it all. Now looking back, I don't know either. I was stretched past what was possible. My body gets tired now and I go to bed. Back then I ignored the signs of my body. I can see now that it's no surprise my body reacted with a tumour. It was literally running on empty. I'm trying to change those old habits every day.

I'm feeling so good, yet there's still this niggling voice in my head that maybe I didn't get it all. I ask for guidance and help as I know I need to consult someone who is not attached to me emotionally, and has had no part in my journey of cancer.

That afternoon I get an email advertising a Journey Intensive weekend workshop in Sydney. I book in without thinking and work out the details as I go, to ensure all are fed and okay while I'm away. I'm so glad to have the opportunity to step out of my life and its demands for a while, to have the space to check in with my body.

I know that the journey process can help me to bypass my ego and connect me directly with my soul. Working with experienced therapists means that I cannot escape from my own wisdom, they should be able to see my subconscious distractions. I meet lovely new people and despite my reservations that I don't need the whole thing, I choose to complete the whole workshop, rather than using the extra time as a meditative retreat. It is so nice to be in a classroom where no one knows me. It is such a luxury to be the student that I stay to enjoy the experience.

I do two very profound journeys with two incredibly gifted women. I'm quick to process, as I can visualise their instructions within seconds. I sink beneath my conscious awareness quickly.

The cancer is confirmed gone and it *has* come as a lesson.

We do extra healing and I once again see the brilliance that is me. I can see I have been born with so many gifts for a reason. I'm here to make a difference with the journey of cancer as one of my tools.

My second journey with the lovely Nikki takes me somewhere deeper again to reawaken my full psychic awareness. I'm so happy and blown away by the process, and I let go of my fears and my shame and the reluctance to embrace my full gifts. As a result, my more than adequate psychic awareness operating at around seven per cent expands out to one hundred per cent. I can see everywhere, see everything; from children playing football in Turkey, to people fighting in Syria, to those snorkelling in the Maldives, to tourists at the top of the Eiffel tower. I can see it as clearly as I can see the keyboard in front of me—there are no filters and no blinkers now. I choose to use it with honour and not as a party trick, and know it will keep me safe as a result.

I didn't need to heal my cancer as I'd already done that, but what I did need to do that weekend was to step out as me.

I needed to walk as Karina Godwin, a wonderful and empowered woman who was kind and generous and loved to a fault. I needed to stand in forgiveness of her failings and to give her a new beginning. I wanted her to have the courage to try and I gave her that.

I returned home happier, confident that I was who I had hoped to be. I realised I had destroyed the girl who had created the tumour. I was a good and beautiful person, and the only value that mattered was the one that I put upon myself.

For the first time, I'm really backing myself. I'm putting myself first in every way and I believe that my visions can come true. I know that my faith in people is warranted, and that if they learn to love themselves, they will not seek or attract conflict with others. I commit to my part in making this real.

Our wishes and manifestations for Berni to be generously paid out to complete his twenty-three years with his company finally come true. My prediction in one of my intuitive course demonstrations several years earlier, has come to fruition. He is now in a position where he can choose what he wants to do.

With six months' garden leave to prevent him working within the industry, he is afforded time to do what he likes. He chooses to give me time to write. It is my turn to be supported to make this next dream come true.

I'm not really going to do anything new. I'm doing what I'm good at and that's getting people to love and care for who they are, to empower them to make choices that put them back in charge of their destiny. I've been teaching them to put themselves first in one way or another for just under fifteen years.

Now I'm so excited to be doing it on a larger scale. I know I'll gain just as much gratitude and be just as humbled by your successes as I am at all of those who have walked my path before you. I hope you'll share your stories and this book with those you love.

I know that you will have success, for I am walking proof of it. I wish you so much love and support and healing upon the way.

I've learnt to live life fully, to live spontaneously and to make memories out of everything. So, when I find myself so advanced in my many projects (the creation of this book, its companion CD, my inspiration cards, *Shine, You Deserve It*, and the four-day self-love healing retreat), we decide to do something crazy. I've always liked to live life as if each day might be my last and cancer has made that even more important. I'm an Adele lover and was so disappointed that I couldn't attend her concerts in Melbourne due to my schedule.

As I sat at a charity dinner with friends on the last night of her Melbourne concerts, I wished I was there. I apologise to Di, and explain that half of me is at the Adele concert. Berni sees my face and tells me to find out where she's going next. He says me that we needn't miss out, we can fly to see her there. When I google the concert, I take a sharp breath. Adele is playing in New Zealand the next weekend. With some clever rescheduling, we find ourselves flying the four hours to Auckland. An hour after landing we are in a cab on the way to the stadium to meet Berni's much loved colleague and his wife, who have two spare tickets in the corporate box for the concert tonight. I am meeting them for the first time, but feel an instant connection. We are having fun well before the concert begins.

Huge storms are forecast and the rain is torrential as the concert begins. Adele is playing a two tier 'round' stage connected by steep stairs. The upper level is undercover, although it isn't protecting her from the rain which is coming in sideways. I look at her as she walks down into that torrential rain and think what a trooper she is. In these conditions, she would have been forgiven for staying where it's dry, but she doesn't seem to care. She shrugs and says she is a Londoner, so she's used to it. Hours of hair and makeup disappear under the torrents of water but still she is singing like the sun is shining. She has the most incredible and powerful voice and barely needs a microphone. I sing and dance away to her music, protected by the awning over the outdoor seating of the box. All we can say about her is *Respect*, with a capital R. She is amazing!

Halfway through the concert, the words of one of her songs hits me and the tears begin to flow. It strikes me that if I hadn't found the tumour when I did, that I could be very, very ill, or even dead. I wouldn't be here for this concert. I look at Adele as she talks of her path through life and her reasons for doing her music. It isn't money or fame; she just wants to do it for the people.

In that moment, I know I have to make my life worthy of those who have not made it through their cancer, or who died before they had their chance to achieve their dreams.

I feel like I represent them all.

I look at Adele and I learn from watching her strength. I am comforted by her ability to face the critics and her fear and do it anyway. I promise myself I'll do it too. Berni sees my tears and matches them with his own when I explain the insight behind them.

We discuss how blessed we are that I'm alive and surrounded by the beautiful family we have. I love them all so much, and my life is so much richer for their presence. I think of my job and how it will expand out globally, and I'm ready and I'm sure. I think of all the support and love I have from my friends and family and know that with it, I'm blessed with the platform to make a difference.

As Adele begins her last song, we stand and Berni pulls me in front of him to wrap me in his arms. I make a memory of that moment. Of life and of being ever so loved. I feel the tones of Adele's voice burying the love into the core of my heart and all of a sudden, a huge bolt of light so filled with love fills me and lights up my body. It's still dark around me, I'm still in Berni's arms and Adele is singing.

I know that something special has just happened. I know what that flash was—I've seen it before when we resuscitate someone with a cardiac arrest—it's the life coming back into their body.

I had just seen my life and my soul come back into me.

I had come full circle and was now the full expression of the brilliance that is me.

Tears are flowing down my face faster than the rain, but everyone is teary or crying. I'm so grateful for this man and the life we have together, for his love and his unconditional support. I look at Berni, I can see his love so clearly. I wonder how I can be so lucky, to be so loved by this man whom I adore and love with the wholeness of my heart. I feel so filled with love, and it just explodes me into such incredible joy.

That's my memory of cancer. It's this moment, the moment I got my life back, the culmination of a journey that had pushed me past my limits. I have come a full circle.

As I look up into Berni's eyes, I know that today is the first day of the rest of my life.

I am on the first day of a new beginning.

Acknowledgements

To my parents and siblings for giving me the beginnings I needed. The lessons you provided and the strengths that came from them have enabled me to grow into a woman who I can be proud of for coping with everything life has thrown at me, thank you! I love you.

To Maddie and Lachy, for being the lights who guided me out of my darkness, thank you. For giving me the reasons to embrace my gifts and for bearing the brunt of having an intuitive mother, you gave me permission to shine the truth of who I am. You are two of my greatest achievements. I love you!

To Berni, words can never express the gratitude and love I have for you. Thank you for embracing my children as your own and for gifting me two more. Your love and support over my journey with cancer can only be measured with the love you gave me when you found me broken and hurting in our beginnings. It is because of you and your faith in me that I can shine so brightly and make my dreams come true. You are my greatest love. I love you more than words can ever express.

To Zavier, for showing me the gifts that are in me, and for being such a loving spirit, thank you. Your willingness to embrace people with such love and kindness has taught me well. You are one of my greatest achievements. I love you.

To Dylan and Elyse, for giving me the privilege of walking alongside you in your lives, for your great hearts and generosity and for allowing your Dad to be so happy with me, thank you. I love you.

To Alesa for your help in the project that has been this book and its companion CD and for all the times you made my work amazing by willingly embracing the work of Meliae and my teaching, thank you. For your friendship and healing during my cancer, I love you.

To John, for your unwavering support, your willingness to drop anything for me and for your willingness to love me so much when you see me so clearly, thank you. For loving me enough to be there for me, vomits and all, during my cancer journey and for your healing, I love you.

To Di, for your constant presence of calm and grounding, and for all that you do to support Flying Souls so that I can do what I do best thank you. For your friendship and honouring me in your marriage, and for your healing and support during my cancer journey, I love you.

To Peta, my oldest friend, for your loyalty and constant friendship and acceptance. Thank you for your healing and support and for being the voice of reason in my cancer journey. I love you.

To the staff of Flying Souls, past and present. Each of you has helped me grow into the woman I am, thank you for the challenges and for the love and support I've had over the years. Without your support of my vision to help the world be a better place, we wouldn't see our clientele walking so brilliantly through their lives. For your love and support during my cancer journey, I love you.

To all of the healing clients and students of Flying Souls that I have treated and taught. Each of you has made a difference in enabling me to facilitate such profound healings and evolve my teaching into such an incredible offering. You're all wonderful, thank you!

To Carolyn, Di, Janette, Merrin, Nat and Sarah for your friendship and support over the past eleven years, it has been invaluable beyond measure. A million breakfasts and birthday celebrations have brought me so much happiness, thank you. I love you!

To our very good friends and family who have brought so much physical and emotional support to my family and I during my cancer journey, I can't thank you enough. You are so many and so precious. If you were invited to the 'Celebrate Your Life' party, know we're talking about you. For the friends who have contributed to my journey, thank you.

To Nanny and Pa for creating a safe haven, for the baking and the lolly jar and for showing me the goodness of who I am, thank you. I love you.

To Joan, for teaching me to speak well, for your love and support during my school years and for welcoming me into your home as one of your own, thank you. Thanks to you, I believe in me.

To Oprah Winfrey for getting me through my darkest days and giving me the example of how to step up and be the real me, I love you!

To Ellen DeGeneres for giving me a shining example of how to be brave, to stand up to those who disagreed and judged and to be me anyway. I love you!

To Rebecca Wylie from Sage Written Word for such sensitivity and positive support during the editing process, thank you. You have helped me to believe that I am born to write.

To Luke for your designs and patience with my multiple projects, thank you.

About the Author

Karina Godwin was born intuitive, with a window into the world that most of us never get to see through. Her healing gifts developed early, culminating in the development of the Meliae Intuitive Healing modality. Her passion for teaching personal growth and meditation led to her founding her healing centre of excellence, Flying Souls Pty Ltd (2003) in Melbourne, Australia. She is revered by many as one of the most gifted healers of our times and has an international clientele from all walks of life. She is married to her soulmate, Berni, and together they have five children.

Recommended

CDs by Karina Godwin

Destiny, Put yourself First Guided Meditations

Dreamland for Kids, Guided Meditations

Meditations to Relax

Meditations for Joy

Meditations for Letting Go

Meditations for Loss

Meditations for Strength

Meditations for Balance

Meditations to Value You

Meditations to Imagine

Inspirational Cards by Karina Godwin

Shine, You Deserve It